LSAT®

PrepTest 84

Unlocked

Deconstructing the June 2018 LSAT

© 2019 by Kaplan, Inc.

Published by Kaplan Publishing, a division of Kaplan, Inc.
750 Third Avenue
New York, NY 10017

ISBN: 978-1-5062-4713-7
10 9 8 7 6 5 4 3 2 1

Table of Contents

The Inside Story

PrepTest 84 was administered in June 2018. It challenged 22,489 test takers. What made this test so hard? Here's a breakdown of what Kaplan students who were surveyed after taking the official exam considered PrepTest 84's most difficult section.

Hardest PrepTest 84 Section as Reported by Test Takers

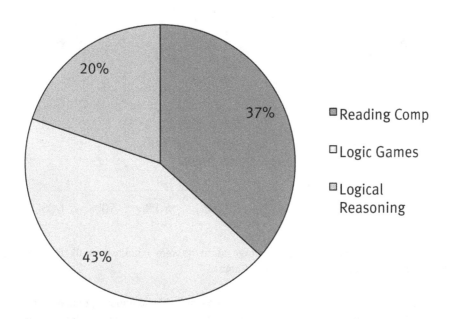

Based on these results, you might think that studying Logic Games is the key to LSAT success. Well, Logic Games is important, but test takers' perceptions don't tell the whole story. For that, you need to consider students' actual performance. The following chart shows the average number of students to miss each question in each of PrepTest 84's different sections.

Percentage Incorrect by PrepTest 84 Section Type

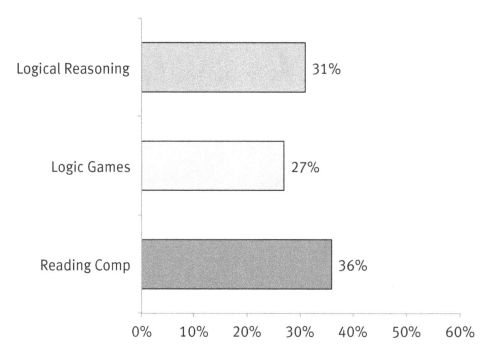

Actual student performance tells quite a different story. On average, students were actually more likely to miss questions in Logical Reasoning and Reading Comprehension than they were in Logic Games.

Maybe students overestimate the difficulty of the Logic Games section because it's so unusual, or maybe it's because a really hard Logic Game is so easy to remember after the test (for instance, this test's final game was very challenging). However, the truth is that the testmaker places hard questions throughout the test. Here were the locations of the 10 hardest (most missed) questions in the exam.

Location of the 10 Most Difficult Questions in PrepTest 84

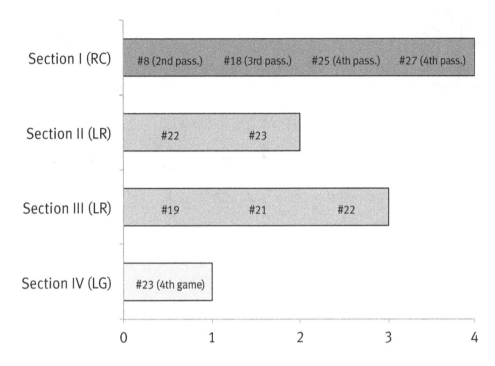

The takeaway from this data is that, to maximize your potential on the LSAT, you need to take a comprehensive approach. Test yourself rigorously, and review your performance on every section of the test. Kaplan's LSAT explanations provide the expertise and insight you need to fully understand your results. The explanations are written and edited by a team of LSAT experts, who have helped thousands of students improve their scores. Kaplan always provides data-driven analysis of the test, ranking the difficulty of every question based on actual student performance. The 10 hardest questions on every test are highlighted with a 4-star difficulty rating, the highest we give. The analysis breaks down the remaining questions into 1-, 2-, and 3-star ratings so that you can compare your performance to thousands of other test takers on all LSAC material.

Don't settle for wondering whether a question was really as hard as it seemed to you. Analyze the test with real data, and learn the secrets and strategies that help top scorers master the LSAT.

7 Can't-Miss Features of PrepTest 84

- 101 questions per test is the standard. However, PrepTest 84 had only 100 questions—the first test to do so since June 2015 (PT 75).
- This was the second PrepTest since June 2007 with no Method of Argument questions. The other test was June 2014 (PT 72).
- The first Logical Reasoning section of PT 84 had two questions about dinosaurs—#13 and #23. Test takers might have recalled those two questions on the Friday night after the test when they were watching the premier of *Jurassic World: Fallen Kingdom*.
- It's not that uncommon to see Strict Sequencing, Matching, Loose Sequencing, or a Hybrid game on a test. But PT 84 was the first test to feature all four since June 2004 (PT 43). Not only did the test feature all those game types, but the Hybrid game was a combination of Distribution and Selection. That means all the common game actions were present on this test.
- Distribution/Selection games are rare—there have only been eight total ever. Prior to PT 84 the most recent ones were in December 2014 (PT 74) (when there were two) and October 2011 (PT 64).
- This was not the test to guess (D) in Logic Games. That answer was only correct twice (tied for the fewest ever)—and both times it was right was on a 1-Star Acceptability question.

- There were only two Detail Questions in the Reading Comp section. There have only been that few three times ever—the two other times were in October 2010 (PT 61) and October 2000 (PT 32).

PrepTest 84 in Context

As much fun as it is to find out what makes a PrepTest unique or noteworthy, it's even more important to know just how representative it is of other LSAT administrations (and, thus, how likely it is to be representative of the exam you will face on Test Day). The following charts compare the numbers of each kind of question and game on PrepTest 84 to the average numbers seen on all officially released LSATs administered over the past five years (from 2013 through 2017).

Number of LR Questions by Type: PrepTest 84 vs. 2013–2017 Average

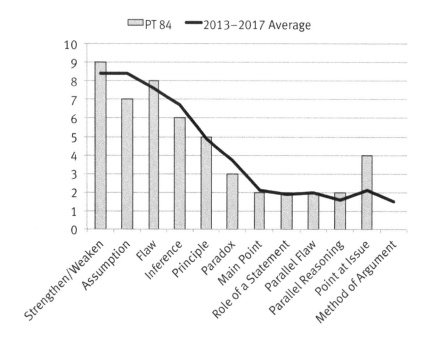

KAPLAN

Number of LG Games by Type: PrepTest 84 vs. 2013–2017 Average

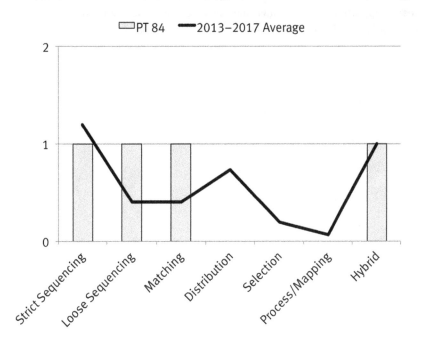

Number of RC Questions by Type: PrepTest 84 vs. 2013–2017 Average

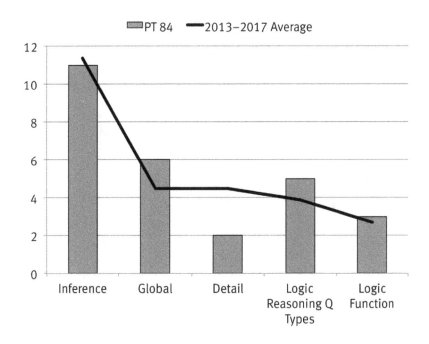

There isn't usually a huge difference in the distribution of questions from LSAT to LSAT, but if this test seems harder (or easier) to you than another you've taken, compare the number of questions of the types on which you, personally, are strongest and weakest. Then, explore within each section to see if your best or worst question types came earlier or later.

Students in Kaplan's comprehensive LSAT courses have access to every released LSAT and to a library of thousands of officially released questions arranged by question, game, and passage type. If you are studying on your own, you have to do a bit more work to identify your strengths and your areas of opportunity. Quantitative analysis (like that in the charts shown here) is an important tool for understanding how the test is constructed, and how you are performing on it.

Section I: Reading Comprehension

Passage 1: Atmospheric Warming and the Greenhouse Effect

Q#	Question Type	Correct	Difficulty
1	Global	D	★★
2	Logic Reasoning (Method of Argument)	C	★★
3	Detail	A	★
4	Inference	E	★★★
5	Logic Function	D	★

Passage 2: Techniques for Police Interviewers

Q#	Question Type	Correct	Difficulty
6	Global	E	★★
7	Detail (EXCEPT)	D	★
8	Logic Function	C	★★★★
9	Inference	A	★★
10	Inference	D	★★★
11	Logic Reasoning (Parallel Reasoning)	B	★★
12	Inference	B	★

Passage 3: The Role of Readers in Classifying Genres

Q#	Question Type	Correct	Difficulty
13	Global	C	★
14	Inference	E	★★
15	Inference	A	★★
16	Logic Reasoning (Method of Argument)	A	★★
17	Inference	A	★★★
18	Inference	B	★★★★
19	Logic Reasoning (Principle)	C	★★

Passage 4: Biological Effect of Cooking Food

Q#	Question Type	Correct	Difficulty
20	Global	B	★★
21	Inference	A	★★
22	Logic Function	B	★
23	Inference	E	★★★
24	Global	E	★★★
25	Logic Reasoning (Strengthen)	B	★★★★
26	Inference	D	★★★
27	Global	D	★★★★

Passage 1: Atmospheric Warming and the Greenhouse Effect

Step 1: Read the Passage Strategically
Sample Roadmap

line #	Keyword/phrase	¶ Margin notes
2	quite compelling	
3	reinforced recently	Definitely warming
10	unprecedented	
11	other recent	
12	strengthened; controversial	
13	Proponents	"Proponents: cause is "greenhouse effect"
14	claim	
17	Early	
18	inconsistent	Early models inconsistent
22	led opponents; question the validity	
23	But new	
24	more acurately	
25	important	
26	overlooked:	New models better: include sulfates
34	consistent	
36	Another question	Alternate explanation: cause is solar variability
42	strong	
44	But	
45	cannot account	
46	While	
51	inevitably reverted	Doesn't fully explain increase
52	But	
53	surpasses	
56	it seems reasonable to conclude	Conclusion; greenhouse explanation more reasonable
59	best	

Discussion

The passage opens with an italicized disclaimer: It was written in the mid-1990s. This author from the distant past starts off by citing *compelling* evidence that temperatures in Earth's atmosphere have been rising—half a degree Celsius over the last 100 years. This temperature rise serves as the **Topic** of the passage. The author then introduces a *controversial* view that this temperature increase is caused by the "greenhouse effect," which involves certain gases preventing heat from leaving the atmosphere. This potential explanation for the rise in temperature serves as the **Scope** of the passage.

In the second paragraph, the author suggests the greenhouse effect explanation was not initially convincing. Early models were not consistent with actual data. *But*, the author then mentions newer models that factor in sulfates, and those models allowed for greater accuracy and consistency. (Did you see all that science-y stuff about volcanoes and solar energy and glacial ice? Notice how utterly unimportant it is for understanding the author's main point.)

The third paragraph introduces another potential pitfall for the greenhouse effect theory. Other scientists argue that Earth's temperatures are actually tied to solar energy variations, not greenhouse gases. According to the author, these scientists have managed to develop some pretty solid models. *But*, the author argues that their models don't match up well with the recent increase, which exceeds even the most drastic fluctuations predicted by the solar energy models.

The author keeps introducing potential objections to the greenhouse effect theory, only to reject those objections and return favor back to the greenhouse effect. Defending that theory serves as the **Purpose** of the passage. And the **Main Idea** is driven home in the very last sentence, when the author says what is "reasonable to conclude" in light of all the evidence: Temperatures have indeed risen, and greenhouse gases offer the best explanation for that.

1. (D) Global

Step 2: Identify the Question Type
The question asks for the "main point of the passage," making this a Global question.

Step 3: Research the Relevant Text
As with any Global question, the entire text is relevant. There's no need to go back into the passage. The main point was predicted when summarizing the big picture.

Step 4: Make a Prediction
The author's main idea, as emphasized in the last line of the passage, is that temperatures have risen, and evidence points to the greenhouse effect theory as the best explanation for that occurrence.

Step 5: Evaluate the Answer Choices
(D) is correct, matching the idea that temperatures have risen, and that there's ample evidence of the greenhouse effect being responsible.

(A) is a 180. The greenhouse effect theory is *supported*, not questioned, by the sulfate data. And the author rejects the idea that solar cycle data refutes the greenhouse effect theory.

(B) is too narrow and a Distortion. This focuses too much on the sulfate data from the second paragraph. Furthermore, the author only talks about how temperatures have risen, not about whether they will continue to rise.

(C) is too narrow. This only refers to the equilibrium temperature information from the third paragraph. Furthermore, although the author does state that the greenhouse effect theory models initially overestimated the temperature increase, new methods have yielded results that are consistent with the temperature increase.

(E) is a Distortion. The author only shows support for the greenhouse effect theory at the end. There's no indication that it needs to be combined with anything else, let alone the inadequate solar-fluctuation theory.

2. (C) Logic Reasoning (Method of Argument)

Step 2: Identify the Question Type
The question asks how the argumentation in the second paragraph relates to that in the third paragraph. Method of Argument questions in Logical Reasoning ask for exactly that: the author's style of argumentation. So, this question will use the exact same skills one would use for such questions in Logical Reasoning, only on a larger scale (due to the size of the paragraphs in Reading Comprehension).

Step 3: Research the Relevant Text
The question is based on understanding *how* the author argues rather than *what* the author says. So, the margin notes should be sufficient for seeing the relationship.

Step 4: Make a Prediction
Both paragraphs are ultimately about the greenhouse effect theory. In the second paragraph, the author describes how early models weren't so great, but newer models are much better. In the third paragraph, the author introduces a potential rival to the greenhouse effect theory, but rejects the rival and claims it's more reasonable to accept the greenhouse effect theory. The correct answer will be consistent with this describe-and-then-defend approach.

Step 5: Evaluate the Answer Choices
(C) is correct. The theory discussed in the second paragraph is the greenhouse effect theory. And the author does accept that theory after weighing considerations (the solar-fluctuation theory) in the third paragraph. The word

tentatively may seem rather weak, but the author does only say that it's *reasonable* to conclude that the greenhouse theory is best. That's not as confident as saying it absolutely *is* the best or that it must be true.

(A) is not accurate. The author only discusses one theory in the second paragraph: the greenhouse effect theory.

(B) is a 180. While there were initially problems with the greenhouse effect theory, the author ultimately shows in the second paragraph that newer models were accurate. And the author goes on to accept that theory *despite* the evidence presented in the third paragraph.

(D) is a Distortion. The author never proposes the greenhouse effect theory personally, and not in the second paragraph. It was introduced in the first paragraph and was already being pushed by proponents. Further, the author never makes any revision to the theory—let alone a *substantial* one.

(E) is a Distortion. The author never questions the validity of the greenhouse effect theory in the second paragraph. In fact, it's the second paragraph in which the theory is shown to be consistent with data. In the third paragraph, the author shows how a competing theory is *not* consistent with recent data.

3. (A) Detail

Step 2: Identify the Question Type
The question asks for something directly "mentioned in the passage," making this a Detail question.

Step 3: Research the Relevant Text
Unfortunately, the stem provides no clues as to where research should be done. The entire text is relevant.

Step 4: Make a Prediction
Through three paragraphs and nearly 60 lines, the author mentioned a lot of details. Predicting the right one would require remarkable clairvoyance. There's no choice but to test the answers individually and research as necessary to make sure the correct answer is directly stated in the passage.

Step 5: Evaluate the Answer Choices
(A) is correct. Sulfates are mentioned in the second paragraph, and the author explains how they affect temperatures in lines 26–30 (they "counteract the heating effect of greenhouse gases by reflecting solar energy back into space").

(B) is Extreme. Sulfates were the overlooked factor that helped make greenhouse effect models finally match data, but that's not to say they are the *main* greenhouse gases.

(C) is never actually mentioned. The third paragraph presents a lot of information about solar cycles and how fluctuations inevitably return to equilibrium. However, there's no mention of an exact time frame for that to happen.

(D) is Out of Scope. The author only discusses the current state and how temperatures are now higher than before. The author never makes any predictions about the future, and glacial ice is never mentioned.

(E) is never mentioned. The author does say that sulfates come from technological sources (line 28), but offers no specific examples. The only example given is a natural source (volcanoes).

4. (E) Inference

Step 2: Identify the Question Type
The question asks for something that can "reasonably be inferred," making this an Inference question.

Step 3: Research the Relevant Text
The question refers to what the author uses to judge a model's success. The author's judgments come primarily in the third paragraph.

Step 4: Make a Prediction
In the third paragraph, the author introduces the solar-fluctuation theory. Like the greenhouse effect theory, the solar-fluctuation theory produced some convincing models. However, in lines 44–55, the author presents the reasoning for judging the solar-fluctuation models as inadequate: The fluctuations in the models just weren't as drastic as the actual change in temperatures. Thus, it can be inferred that anticipating such changes is a vital factor in judging a model's success.

Step 5: Evaluate the Answer Choices
(E) matches the prediction and is correct.

(A) is a Distortion. Both the greenhouse effect theory and the solar-fluctuation theory produce models that correspond well with temperature observations. The author ultimately rejects the solar-fluctuation models because they were unable to anticipate the drastic *change* (or fluctuations) in temperature (lines 52–55).

(B) is Out of Scope. The author never suggests that any theory has a "simple explanatory framework."

(C) is a Distortion. In the second paragraph, the greenhouse effect theory was revised to account for sulfates. However, there is no suggestion that experimental findings were the cause of that revision. And even if they were, it wasn't the deciding factor that swayed the author in the third paragraph.

(D) is not supported. The author's judgments are based on how well the models fit temperature data, not about the warming mechanisms they describe.

5. (D) Logic Function

Step 2: Identify the Question Type
The question asks for the author's *purpose* in including certain text. That makes this a Logic Function question. Even though the wording says "primary purpose," this is not a Global question, because it asks about the purpose of a

specific set of lines rather than the purpose of the entire passage.

Step 3: Research the Relevant Text

The question asks about lines 26–35, but be sure to consider the context of the surrounding lines. The purpose of those lines should also be consistent with the entire paragraph in which they appear, so use your margin notes to get a bigger sense of the purpose.

Step 4: Make a Prediction

The lines in question discuss sulfates, how they affect temperatures, and how factoring them in made newer greenhouse effect models more accurate. This was a major turning point in the paragraph, as the first half talked about how earlier greenhouse effect models were rejected by opponents as inconsistent. So, the purpose of lines 26–35 is to provide the information that shows how newer models were able to overcome the questions of validity that opponents had.

Step 5: Evaluate the Answer Choices

(D) is correct. Opponents did have doubts about the greenhouse effect theory (lines 21–23), and the additional data about sulfates provided a solid defense in favor of the greenhouse effect theory.

(A) is a Distortion. The lines discuss sulfates, which helped the greenhouse effect models match observations. However, the author provides no specific set of observations that were predicted.

(B) is Out of Scope. The author never calls for a new theory to be formulated.

(C) is a 180. The greenhouse effect theory had previously been questioned by opponents, and this data regarding sulfates is the evidence that shows how new models *do* match observed phenomena.

(E) is a Distortion. A competing theory (the solar-fluctuation theory) isn't brought up until the next paragraph. The lines in question are only used in reference to one theory: the greenhouse effect theory.

Passage 2: Techniques for Police Interviewers

Step 1: Read the Passage Strategically
Sample Roadmap

line #	Keyword/phrase	¶ Margin notes
1		Police want info
5	One method	Cognitive interview
16–17	general consensus; proven successful	works well
18	little impact	
19	incorrect	
20	However; problem	But…
23	Because	problems
25	even	
27	alternative	Alternative:
28	Indeed	hypnosis
29	However	
30	even though; much less	
31	evidence suggests	
33–34	not generally improved; in fact; may deteriorate; may also	Easier, but not more accurate
38	difficulties; most notably	Other problems
40	ideal	Ideal
47	may in fact	
49	both	Solution: close eyes
50	Recent	
51	can benefit	
54	indicate; improvement	Studies support
55	no problems	
57	More significantly	
59	equivalent	As good as cognitive interview
60	And	
61	no; no	
62	no	

KAPLAN

Discussion

The passage opens with the police's goal in interviewing witnesses: Get as much information as possible. The author then introduces one method for achieving this goal: a cognitive interview. This sets up the **Topic** (interviewing witnesses). However, with a such a short opening, it's hard to know if the passage will focus entirely on the cognitive interview. So, move on for now, but anticipate some explanation of the cognitive interview along with an evaluation of that method.

Sure enough, the author provides all of that in the second paragraph. It describes the cognitive interview, which combines cognitive techniques (memory recall) and communication techniques (effective conversation). Then, the author provides evaluation. Generally, the cognitive interview is considered successful; witnesses provide more details with equal accuracy. *However*, there are problems. The method is complex, requires a lot of training, and even trained officers stray from the method.

In the third paragraph, the author introduces an alternative method: hypnosis. Although not nearly as complex as the cognitive interview, the author wastes no time presenting the problems with hypnosis. It doesn't improve accuracy, it gives witnesses false confidence, and some people are not susceptible to hypnosis.

In the last paragraph, the author describes a magical ideal—a method that requires no training, could be used on anyone, and would lead to more information without creating greater inaccuracy. And the author suggests such a method exists. It's called "instructed eye-closure." In other words, you just tell witnesses to close their eyes. And research suggests this works! The rest of the paragraph describes how this method fits the ideal described at the beginning of the paragraph.

The **Scope** of the passage focuses on various methods for interviewing witnesses. The **Purpose** is to introduce and evaluate these methods. And the **Main Idea** is that, of the methods discussed, telling witnesses to close their eyes seems to be the ideal way for police to get the information they want.

6. (E) Global

Step 2: Identify the Question Type
The question asks for the "main point" of the entire passage, making this a Global question.

Step 3: Research the Relevant Text
As Global questions ask about the entire passage, everything is relevant. Instead of going back into the details, use the Main Idea as predicted while reading the passage.

Step 4: Make a Prediction
The author's main point comes at the end: While the cognitive interview and hypnosis are problematic, simply telling

witnesses to close their eyes offers an ideal way for police to get the details they want.

Step 5: Evaluate the Answer Choices
(E) is correct. It doesn't mention the problematic methods of the cognitive interview and hypnosis. However, it doesn't need to. It focuses on the ultimate point about eye-closure being the ideal solution to getting more information from witnesses.

(A) is too narrow. It does a nice job of summarizing the ideal described at the beginning of the last paragraph. However, it fails to mention that such an ideal may exist: having witnesses close their eyes.

(B) is a 180. In the last paragraph, it's suggested that having witnesses close their eyes can work without requiring any such trade-off between reliability and practicality.

(C) is too narrow. While the author does say that instructed eye-closure exists in the cognitive interview and hypnosis (lines 48–50), this misses the point that having witnesses close their eyes can be an ideal method for getting information.

(D) is a 180. By the end, the author is pushing eye closure, not the cognitive interview. In fact, the author claims that having witnesses close their eyes can be just as effective as the cognitive interview (lines 57–60).

7. (D) Detail (EXCEPT)

Step 2: Identify the Question Type
The question asks for information that "is true" "[a]ccording to the passage," making this a Detail question. However, take note of the EXCEPT, which means the correct answer will be the only choice that is *not* necessarily true.

Step 3: Research the Relevant Text
The question asks about the instructed eye-closure technique, which is described throughout the last paragraph.

Step 4: Make a Prediction
There are a lot of details about the eye-closure technique, making it difficult to predict which ones will populate the wrong choices. And there are infinite details that are *not* mentioned, so predicting the correct answer will be impossible. Instead, keep in mind the big picture about the eye-closure technique: It's pretty much ideal. If a detail looks unfamiliar, you can always go back to the last paragraph to double check. The correct answer will not be mentioned or will contradict the passage. Or, because the passage brings up several methods of interviewing witnesses, it's reasonable to expect the correct answer to misapply a detail from the passage that actually applies to a different method.

Step 5: Evaluate the Answer Choices
(D) is correct, as this is a detail about hypnosis (line 35), not the eye-closure technique.

(A) is mentioned in line 60, which claims that the eye-closure technique requires "no specialist training," and no training is certainly less than the "substantial training" (line 22) required by the cognitive interview method.

(B) is mentioned in lines 50–53.

(C) is mentioned in lines 60–61 ("no increase in errors").

(D) is mentioned in lines 48–50.

8. (C) Logic Function

Step 2: Identify the Question Type
The phrase "in order to" indicates the question is asking *why* the author mentions alibis, making this a Logic Function question.

Step 3: Research the Relevant Text
The question directs you to the first sentence. Given that the scope changes in the next sentence, the first sentence alone should be sufficient for answering this question.

Step 4: Make a Prediction
The first sentence introduces the goal of interviewing witnesses: get more information. This information can be used to confirm or dismiss alibis. Thus, the mention of alibis is meant to show a benefit the police gain from the information gathered during the interview process.

Step 5: Evaluate the Answer Choices
(C) is correct. Confirming or denying alibis is mentioned as a use for the information gathered in an interview.

(A) is a Faulty Use of Detail. Psychologists and research are not mentioned until later paragraphs, and not in any direct connection to evaluating alibis.

(B) is Out of Scope. The police are trying to elicit information from *witnesses* that could be used to confirm or deny alibis. They are not seeking to elicit the alibis themselves from the *suspects*.

(D) is a Distortion. Psychologists are not mentioned until the second paragraph, and the author never tries to contrast their concerns with those of the police.

(E) is a Faulty Use of Detail. The cognitive interview is not mentioned in the first sentence, and the reasons for its complexity are not brought up until halfway through the second paragraph. And even then, alibis have nothing to do with the complexity.

9. (A) Inference

Step 2: Identify the Question Type
The correct answer will be something with which the author is "most likely to agree," making this an Inference question.

Step 3: Research the Relevant Text
The question offers no specific references, so the entire text is relevant.

Step 4: Make a Prediction
The correct answer could come from anywhere in the passage, so an exact prediction will not be possible. Instead, stick to the big picture (eye-closure technique is good; other techniques are problematic), and only research answer choices as necessary to confirm or eliminate.

Step 5: Evaluate the Answer Choices
(A) is correct. This is supported in the last sentence of the second paragraph (lines 24–26), in which deviation from training is presented as a potential problem with the cognitive interview method.

(B) is Extreme. Building rapport is said to be part of the cognitive interview process (lines 13–15). However, success is not said to be *largely* derived from this ability. In fact, the potentially equally successful method of eye closure is not said to require any sort of rapport.

(C) is Out of Scope. The only benefit of hypnosis mentioned in the passage is in lines 30–31 (it's not as complex as the cognitive interview). No mention is made of how much training might be required to perform hypnosis.

(D) is a 180. Lines 50–54 suggest that the eye-closure technique can be effective for both auditory and visual information. There would be no need to use multiple techniques.

(E) is not supported. While complexity is a drawback of the cognitive interview, there's no suggestion that complexity affects the accuracy. In fact, the author even claims that the cognitive interview does *not* affect accuracy (lines 19–20).

10. (D) Inference

Step 2: Identify the Question Type
The question asks for something that can be "inferred from the passage," making this an Inference question.

Step 3: Research the Relevant Text
The question asks about potential consequences of hypnosis, which are laid out in lines 31–39 in the third paragraph.

Step 4: Make a Prediction
According to the third paragraph, accuracy is not improved with hypnosis and may actually deteriorate. Also, it can create "false confidence" (i.e., witnesses appear more confident, even when their information is wrong). The correct answer will be consistent with this drop in accuracy or increased confidence in false information.

Step 5: Evaluate the Answer Choices
(D) is correct. When witness have "false confidence," they will be confident about their responses, even when they're wrong. That means confidence will not be a reliable indicator of accuracy.

(A) is a Distortion. This confuses percentages and numbers. By lines 31–34, the *proportion* (or percentage) of accurate responses may go down. However, that could be from 80 percent accurate to 60 percent accurate. A lower percentage, but still more accurate than inaccurate.

(B) is a Distortion of a couple of facts. First, it's the witnesses that get overconfident, not the interviewers. Second, it's the cognitive interview that's described as complex, not hypnosis.

(C) is Out of Scope. There is no mention made about witnesses *intentionally* trying to deceive the interviewer, or the ability of interviewers to detect such deception.

(E) is a Distortion. The author does mention that some witnesses may not be susceptible to hypnosis (lines 38–39), but there is no suggestion that people become less susceptible over time, or that such susceptibility leads to a drop in information provided.

11. (B) Logic Reasoning (Parallel Reasoning)

Step 2: Identify the Question Type
The question asks for a relationship "most analogous" to one presented in the passage. That makes this a Parallel Reasoning question, similar to those found in the Logical Reasoning section.

Step 3: Research the Relevant Text
Any relationship between the cognitive interview process and the eye-closure technique will be in the third paragraph. And that happens in lines 48–50.

Step 4: Make a Prediction
In lines 48–50, the author claims that the eye-closure technique is actually part of the cognitive interview process. While the cognitive interview process surely involves a lot more (it is described as complex), closing one's eyes is still part of it. So the relationship is that one technique is actually part of the other, more involved technique. The correct answer will describe two other concepts with the same relationship: one being part of the other.

Step 5: Evaluate the Answer Choices
(B) is correct. This describes two effective methods for producing health benefits, and one (increasing fiber) is part of the other (increasing fiber *and* reducing fat).

(A) does not match. This describes two methods that are opposite one another: one that involves light exercise, and one that involves strenuous exercise.

(C) does not match. This describes two completely different methods that produce two different results (moderate caffeine is healthy, while excessive caffeine is not).

(D) does not match. It only provides one approach (taking a new vitamin supplement) and showing a different effect on two separate groups (men versus women).

(E) does not match. This does provide one method (exercise alone) that is part of the other (diet and exercise). However, the exercise alone is said to be *less* effective here, while the eye-closure alone was said to be equally effective (lines 57–60) in the passage.

12. (B) Inference

Step 2: Identify the Question Type
The question asks for something with which the author is "most likely to agree," making this an Inference question.

Step 3: Research the Relevant Text
The question provides no specific references or Content Clues, so the entire text is relevant.

Step 4: Make a Prediction
There are too many possible inferences to choose from, so don't bother going back into the text. Stick to the main themes (eye-closure good; other methods flawed), and test choices against the passage as necessary.

Step 5: Evaluate the Answer Choices
(B) is correct. In lines 20–23, the complexity of the cognitive interview is based on both the substantial training *and* the length of time it takes to conduct such an interview. So, even if the police did have the time and resources to complete the training, that wouldn't change the problem that the interview is a long process.

(A) is not supported, and likely a 180. Even if everybody *were* susceptible to hypnosis, it would still have the problems outlined in lines 29–37 (potentially lower accuracy and creation of "false confidence").

(C) is not supported. Even if the police *did* have the resources, the author might still suggest the eye-closure method, as it could be equally effective (lines 57–60).

(D) is not supported. The three theories presented are not enough to warrant such an absolute correlation between difficulty and accuracy. Besides, even if eye-closure is considered "easy to learn" and the cognitive interview is considered "difficult to learn," the author suggests they can produce an equal amount of accurate info (lines 57–60). The *easy* method wouldn't necessarily produce more.

(E) is not supported. "False confidence" is said to arise from hypnosis, but it's never said such confidence increases based on how much information the witness provides.

Passage 3: The Role of Readers in Classifying Genres

Step 1: Read the Passage Strategically
Sample Roadmap

line #	Keyword/phrase	¶ Margin notes
Passage A		
2		Borges: detective novel created specific readers
7	any	
10	but	Author: insight into lit
11	insight	
15	suggests	Borges: lit requires reader
18	not; but instead; essential	
19	Thus	Auth: genres based on readers, not formal elements
20	rather than	
Passage B		
23	but	Genres can be based on themes, but...
24	difficulties	
25	notorious	
27–28	fails; more fruitful	
30	:	better to use reading protocols
33	But; most central	
34	clearly	
38	major; must therefore	Critics should study what creates reading protocol
42	example	
44	:	ex: poetry
46	Therefore	
48		ex: science fiction
51	Therefore	

Discussion

Passage A opens with an observation from Jorge Luis Borges, who claims that detective novels have created a particular type of reader. These readers learn to read any literature with disbelief and skepticism. The author goes on to say that Borges's observations can provide insight into literature in general.

In the second paragraph, the author presents further claims from Borges that reading is an aesthetic experience that requires combining the reader and text. It is essential for readers, in some way, to participate in the process. *Thus*, the author concludes that genres are determined based on how the stories are read rather than the formal literary elements.

The **Topic** of passage A is literature, focusing on the **Scope** of the reader's experience with literature. The **Purpose** is mostly informative with the **Main Idea** that, as illustrated by detective stories and their readers, literature requires a combination of reader participation and text, and that's what helps classify a work's genre.

The author of passage B jumps right into a discussion of genre classification. The author claims that genres can be defined by thematic elements, but (foreshadowing some common ground with passage A) such an approach can be problematic. Some books blur the lines and don't easily fit one category. The author then offers a "more fruitful" approach to classification based on reading protocols, i.e., how people read and respond to the material. This sounds a lot like the ideas proposed at the end of passage A.

Still in the first paragraph, the author admits that people can read books any way they want. However, texts of certain genres are written so that the experience is enhanced if read a particular way.

In the second paragraph, the author concludes (*therefore*) that critical interpretation should focus on rhetorical devices that affect one's reading protocol. The author supports this with examples about poetry (the protocol is to listen to the sounds of words, so critics should focus on such auditory devices) and science fiction (the protocol is to experience alternative worlds, so critics should focus on devices that differentiate our world from the one in the story).

The **Topic** of passage B is fiction writing and the **Scope** is classifying genres through reading protocols. The **Purpose** is to advocate the **Main Idea**: to properly classify genres of fiction, critics should focus on the rhetorical devices that contribute to the reading protocol.

Both passages go off on tangents regarding different genres (passage A spends a lot of time on detective stories, while passage B brings up examples of poetry and science fiction). However, it's useful to note that both passages ultimately reach a conclusion about using the way people read stories to determine genre. In that sense, the general principle underlying each passage is very similar.

13. (C) Global

Step 2: Identify the Question Type
The question asks for something both passages are "concerned with answering." That will comprise the overall purpose of each passage, making this a Global question.

Step 3: Research the Relevant Text
As with any Global question, the entire text is relevant. Focus on the Purpose and Main Idea of each passage, as determined while reading strategically.

Step 4: Make a Prediction
While both passages have their individual tangents, they both ultimately come around to the same idea: In classifying a work's genre, it's important to consider how people read the story rather than the literary elements. The correct answer should be a question regarding the classification of writings.

Step 5: Evaluate the Answer Choices
(C) is correct, as both passages answer this question by saying classification of genre is based on the way people read the works.

(A) is Out of Scope. Neither passage questions the literary value of any particular genres.

(B) is only brought up in passage A, in which Borges credits Poe with creating the detective story. The author of passage B never mentions detective stories or who created them.

(D) is Out of Scope. Both passages claim that genre is determined by reader activity, not by the author. There is no mention in either passage of what role the author plays.

(E) is Out of Scope. Neither passage compares these genres. Besides, only passage A mentions detective fiction, and only passage B mentions science fiction.

14. (E) Inference

Step 2: Identify the Question Type
The correct answer will be something about which both authors are "most likely to agree," making this an Inference question.

Step 3: Research the Relevant Text
The question offers no specific references or Content Clues, so the entire text is relevant. Instead, consider big picture ideas about which both passages agree.

Step 4: Make a Prediction
While an exact prediction may be difficult, remember that both passages share a common theme. They both agree that classifying a work's genre involves how the work is read rather than standard literary elements. Any answer that is consistent with that idea should be a winner.

Step 5: Evaluate the Answer Choices

(E) is correct. Both authors argue that genres are based on how readers read the works. So, even if the formal elements are the same (e.g., plot, settings), two books can be of different genres if they are expected to be read in different ways.

(A) is Out of Scope. Neither passage makes any distinction between short and long works of fiction. (And even if you consider *poetry* short, the author of passage B suggests in line 42 that poetry is not actually considered *fiction*.)

(B) is Out of Scope. Passage A mentions Poe writing the first detective story. However, no motive is provided, and passage B makes no mention of the first science fiction story.

(C) is Extreme and a 180. Both passages show distaste for using formal elements to demarcate the boundaries of genres, but neither says there is *no* value in doing so. Besides, they *do* suggest demarcating boundaries. They just encourage using reading protocols instead of formal elements.

(D) is Out of Scope. Neither passage brings up literary value, nor does either one address defying conventions.

15. (A) Inference

Step 2: Identify the Question Type

The question asks for the stance taken by the author of passage A. This is an Author's Attitude question, which is a subset of Inference questions. The author's stance will not be directly stated, but will be inferred by the language of the passage.

Step 3: Research the Relevant Text

Borges's views are all over passage A, as are the author's views. So, the entire text is relevant.

Step 4: Make a Prediction

The author never uses any Keywords to specifically evaluate Borges's claims. However, the author's views are consistent with Borges's views, and the author even uses Borges's views to bolster the main point. That, at the very least, suggests a strong level of agreement.

Step 5: Evaluate the Answer Choices

(A) is correct. While the author never directly commends Borges's views, the author's use of Borges's views to further the main idea of the passage suggests nothing less than full agreement.

(B) is a Distortion. The author never expresses any reluctance or hesitancy in accepting Borges's views.

(C) is a Distortion. The author's use of Borges's views implies more approval than neutrality. Besides, there is no caution on the author's part.

(D) is a 180. The author's views are consistent with Borges's. There is no sense of skepticism.

(E) is a 180. The author's views are in sync with Borges's. There is no evidence that the author would reject anything Borges said.

16. (A) Logic Reasoning (Method of Argument)

Step 2: Identify the Question Type

The question asks for the "argumentative structures" of the passages, making this a Method of Argument question like those found in Logical Reasoning.

Step 3: Research the Relevant Text

Because the question asks about the structures of the entire passages, all of the text is relevant. However, the question is about *how* the passages are structured rather than the content, so consult your margin notes to see how all of the information is organized.

Step 4: Make a Prediction

Passage A starts out with information about detective novels that is then expanded upon to apply to all literature. Passage B jumps right in with a discussion of fiction, in general, and then provides specific examples to back up the main idea. Expect the correct answer to play off these reversed structures.

Step 5: Evaluate the Answer Choices

(A) is correct. Passage A moves from specific (detective novels) to general, while passage B goes from general ideas to specific (poetry and science fiction).

(B) immediately distorts passage A. The views of Borges in passage A are consistent with the author's, not competing.

(C) is Out of Scope for passage A. All of the views presented in passage A are consistent with, not counter to, the author's views. Further, passage B has no counterexamples, either.

(D) is Out of Scope. Neither passage brings up any contradictions that need to be resolved.

(E) is Out of Scope. Neither passage begins with any thought experiments.

17. (A) Inference

Step 2: Identify the Question Type

The question asks for something with which the author of passage B is "most likely to agree," making this an Inference question.

Step 3: Research the Relevant Text

The question only asks about passage B, so only that passage is relevant. However, without any further clues, there is no way to research anything specifically. Instead, focus on the big picture.

Step 4: Make a Prediction

Keep in mind that passage B encourages the use of reading protocols to classify works of fiction. The correct answer should be consistent with that point of view. Only research choices as necessary to confirm there is direct support for the correct answer.

Step 5: Evaluate the Answer Choices

(A) is supported. According to lines 33–35, the texts "most central" to a genre are those written to exploit a specific protocol. That suggests the ones *not* written to exploit a protocol are not most central to the genre, and thus more likely to be a "borderline case," as described earlier in the paragraph.

(B) is a 180, at worst. The principle in passage B is that genre classification is based on the reader's experience, so it seems contradictory to suggest that reader expectations are not essential.

(C) is a 180. Passage B starts off by saying that one *can* use thematic similarities to classify genres. However, the author immediately expresses problems with that idea and presents a "more fruitful" method starting in line 27.

(D) is a 180. The reading protocols that define genres according to passage B include the ways in which readers respond to and make sense of individual sentences (lines 30–32)

(E) is a 180, at worst. The point of passage B is that genre classification shouldn't be based on themes and other literary elements. It should be based on the reading protocols. So, some books in a genre may have completely different themes but the same reading protocol.

18. (B) Inference

Step 2: Identify the Question Type

The question asks for something about which Borges (from passage A) and the author of passage B are "most likely to agree." That makes this an Inference question.

Step 3: Research the Relevant Text

Borges's views are throughout passage A, and passage B consists entirely of the author's views. That makes almost all of the text relevant. It's best to look at the individual views of Borges, rather than the views of passage A's author. Then, consider which views are consistent with passage B, and use that as a prediction.

Step 4: Make a Prediction

In the first paragraph of passage A, Borges claims that detective novels have created special readers who now read any literature with the same incredulous, suspicious eye. In the second paragraph, Borges pushes that literature is an "aesthetic event" that marries the reader and the text. The views of passage B are consistent with both of these ideas, so look for an answer that matches at least one.

Step 5: Evaluate the Answer Choices

(B) is correct. Borges suggests that the readers of detective stories will now read any narrative as if it were a detective story (lines 5–8). And the author of passage B verifies this in lines 32–33 by saying people can read any text in any way they want.

(A) is Extreme. To both Borges and the author of passage B, the genre is dependent on the reader's protocol and is not *fully* determined by the author's intention.

(C) is Extreme. In passage B, the author suggests that the texts "most central to a genre" will be clearly classified. However, there could still be some texts that are not central and still on the borderline.

(D) is Out of Scope for Borges, who never discusses poetry versus prose, and Extreme for passage B. Passage B only says that we pay more attention to certain figures in poetry than we do in prose. That does not mean such figures *never* appear in prose.

(E) is Extreme. Knowing the genre and reading the story with a particular reading protocol will certainly create a more rewarding experience, but that doesn't mean readers won't enjoy the story at all otherwise.

19. (C) Logic Reasoning (Principle)

Step 2: Identify the Question Type

This question requires two steps. First, identify the principle underlying the views in passage B. Then, take the principle and apply it to the views of Borges from passage A. This is similar to how Parallel Principle questions work in Logical Reasoning, and the same approach to such questions will be used here.

Step 3: Research the Relevant Text

The question is based on views that are spread throughout both passages, so practically the entire text is relevant. Focus on the big picture to predict the broader themes being discussed.

Step 4: Make a Prediction

Start by considering the Main Idea of passage B, which is that genre classification should be based on the rhetorical devices that contribute to that genre's reading protocol. That in itself is a general idea, and thus serves as a good principle. Now, that needs to be applied to Borges's views on detective fiction. According to Borges, detective novel readers approach stories with "incredulity and suspicions" (lines 5–8). So, taking the general rule of passage B and applying the specific content from passage A, that means a work classified as detective fiction should have rhetorical devices that contribute to readers being incredulous and suspicious as they read.

Step 5: Evaluate the Answer Choices

(C) is a perfect match to the prediction.

(A) is Out of Scope. The principle of passage B is based on how the story is read, not what types of characters are included in the story.

(B) is Out of Scope. The principle is that stories need to be read a certain way. They don't need to reflect social concerns.

(D) is a 180. Both Borges and the author of passage B suggest that genres do not have to conform to certain thematic elements (e.g., puzzles to be unraveled).

(E) is Out of Scope. The author of passage B does not pass judgment on any genre classification, let alone detective fiction. Further, this does not apply to the views of Borges, who is just fine with how the classification of detective fiction is defined.

Passage 4: Biological Effect of Cooking Food

Step 1: Read the Passage Strategically
Sample Roadmap

line #	Keyword/phrase	¶ Margin notes
1	might reasonably have been expected	might expect cooking didn't change anatomy
3–4	After all	
6	However	
7	only	However, no more raw diet
10	Important; obstacles	
13	suggest	Humans evolved to need cooked food
16–17	Furthermore; widespread assumption	
19	appears to be wrong	
22	implication	
25	suggest	can't survive on raw
26	led to inability	
28	Important questions therefore arise	why no more raw?
30	prinicipal	
34	suggest; consequence	smaller teeth/jaws
38	also possible	
42	If so	Cooking food can explain this evolution
43	may prove to result from	
47	harder; because	Evolution of soft parts harder to confirm
54	however; may therefore; at least	Because of high raw-meat diet or cooking?
55	as well explained	
58	therefore warranted	Need more tests

Discussion

The passage opens with an idea that "might reasonably be expected." That sounds like an idea waiting to be rejected by the authors (yes, plural—see the repeated use of *we* in lines 25 and 33). And sure enough, rejecting that claim is exactly what the entire passage is about.

The supposedly reasonable idea is that adopting the ability to cook food should have had no effect on human anatomy. *However*, by as early as line 6, the authors provide evidence for why that idea may be wrong. Our bodies *have* changed. Except in rare circumstances, our bodies have now evolved to eat only food that is easily chewed and digestible. *Furthermore*, cooking food helps us eat high-calorie diets more efficiently, and the authors suggest this is why we can no longer survive on raw food diets.

In just one paragraph, the big picture of the entire passage is revealed. The **Topic** is cooking food. The **Scope** is what evolutionary effect, if any, cooking has had on human anatomy. The **Purpose** is to present evidence in favor of the authors' **Main Idea**, which is that cooking food may indeed be responsible for the human body evolving. The rest of the passage just provides additional support and details about this phenomenon.

The second paragraph discusses the question of why our bodies can no longer handle as much raw food. It's mentioned that our teeth and jaws started getting smaller around 100,000 years ago. The authors of course suggest this is a consequence of eating cooked food. They also claim that later variations to teeth and jaws occurred as cooking methods improved. To further this claim, they suggest that tooth and jaw size may have started shrinking due to cooking as early as 1.9 million years ago, and that new cooking methods (such as boiling) could be responsible for the further shrinking from 100,000 years ago.

The final paragraph is important because the authors do finally admit that their point of view isn't entirely verified. There are some parts of our anatomy (the soft parts, e.g., the gut, the intestines) that are harder to study. It's possible that our digestive anatomy is actually adapted to a raw meat diet (which would run contrary to the authors' view), but the authors claim it's just as likely that our anatomy is adapted to a high caloric density diet and thus explained by our adoption of cooking food (which would support the authors' view). The authors admit that further testing is warranted. So, their view still needs a little more support, but they're holding steadfast to the idea that our bodies are now adapted to eating cooked food.

20. (B) Global

Step 2: Identify the Question Type
The question asks for the "main point" of the entire passage, making this a Global question.

Step 3: Research the Relevant Text
Global questions ask about the entire passage, so all of the text is relevant. Don't go back into the details. Use the Main Idea as predicted while reading the passage.

Step 4: Make a Prediction
The authors' Main Idea is that the human body may have evolved because of our adoption of cooking food.

Step 5: Evaluate the Answer Choices
(B) is a match. Note how this answer isn't too strong, only suggesting that there's evidence to support the authors' views. This is important because the last paragraph suggests more testing needs to be done, so the answer to a main point question couldn't have been any stronger.

(A) is too narrow. The loose language in the second and third paragraphs suggests this choice is accurate—there is no clear resolution to certain questions. However, this completely misses the authors' point, which is that our adoption of cooking food may be the answer.

(C) is too narrow, focusing only on the details about teeth and jaws from the second paragraph. It also strays from the Scope of the passage, which is about cooking food being the cause.

(D) is too narrow and a Faulty Use of Detail. The time frame of 250,000 years is a reference to the fire and ovens mentioned in lines 19–22. However, the authors suggest that cooking food may have started as early as 1.9 million years ago (lines 38–41). Besides, the passage is focused on how cooking food affected our anatomy, not when it started to happen.

(E) is a 180, at worst. The authors are suggesting that our bodies *did* biologically adapt to eating cooked food. Besides, whether or not such adaptation was necessary is Out of Scope of the passage.

21. (A) Inference

Step 2: Identify the Question Type
The correct answer here will be something with which the authors are "most likely to agree," making this an Inference question.

Step 3: Research the Relevant Text
With no Content Clues or specific references, the entire text is relevant.

Step 4: Make a Prediction
A specific prediction will not be possible here. Instead, look for choices that stick to the bigger themes (humans started cooking food, our bodies evolved, and we can no longer eat

raw food), and use clues in the choices to do any necessary research.

Step 5: Evaluate the Answer Choices

(A) is correct. This is supported in the second paragraph, which raises the question of what limits our ability to utilize raw food. And that's when the authors discuss the evolution of smaller teeth and jaws.

(B) is not supported. The only reference to *Homo ergaster* is in lines 38–41. However, the lines only talk about the jaw and tooth size. There is no indication of the diet or intestine size of this human ancestor.

(C) is a 180, at worst. The only reference to eating plants is in line 12, which suggests that we couldn't live in the wild today because our bodies would have a tough time digesting raw plants. However, that's a modern evolution. If anything, this suggests that our ancestors *did* eat raw plants, and our bodies have changed because we now cook our food.

(D) is a 180. In the last paragraph, the authors do suggest that people traditionally believed this claim (lines 48–50). However, the authors then counter that by asserting their own, equally possible view—those features instead adapted due to our adoption of cooking food (lines 52–56).

(E) is not supported. There is no indication how much our anatomy has changed, but the authors present enough information to suggest it's more than just a *little*.

22. (B) Logic Function

Step 2: Identify the Question Type
The question asks for the "primary purpose" of a claim in the first paragraph. Because it's asking for the purpose of one particular portion and not the entire passage, this is a Logic Function question.

Step 3: Research the Relevant Text
The parenthetical statement in question is in lines 19–22. Be sure to read the surrounding text and look for Keywords to understand the purpose of that claim.

Step 4: Make a Prediction
Directly before the parenthetical is a strong opinion. The authors claim that people are wrong to believe that the practice of cooking is too recent to have had an evolutionary impact. The parenthetical goes on to reference evidence of ovens from 250,000 years ago. So, the purpose of that evidence is to show how cooking is *not* too recent an event and *could* have impacted our evolution, despite what some naysayers would believe.

Step 5: Evaluate the Answer Choices
(B) is correct. It shows that cooking is not a recent phenomenon and may have been around a lot longer than some people believe.

(A) is a Distortion. The parenthetical suggests that 250,000 years is ample time for something to impact our biological evolution. However, that doesn't mean such a long period of time is *required*. Perhaps we only need 50,000 years, and 250,000 years was more than enough time. There is no indication what the cutoff requirement is.

(C) is a Distortion. The parenthetical does provide a time and a place. However, that's just some of the earliest evidence of ovens. Humans may have started cooking food more often back then, but the evolution to being unable to survive on raw-food diets may not have taken place until much later.

(D) is a 180. There are people who agree with this and want to undercut the connection between cooking food and our anatomy. They're the ones who claim we started cooking our food too recently. However, the parenthetical claim in question is meant to contradict those people, and hence this answer choice.

(E) is a Distortion. The parenthetical does mention the technology (if you want to call it that) of "earth ovens." However, that's not the purpose of the claim. The claim is meant to reject the view that we started cooking food too recently. The authors are not interested in discussing the technology used in cooking food.

23. (E) Inference

Step 2: Identify the Question Type
The question asks for something with which the authors are "most likely to agree," making this an Inference question.

Step 3: Research the Relevant Text
With no Content Clues or reference points, the entire passage is relevant. Use the big picture summary as a guideline to start testing answer choices.

Step 4: Make a Prediction
As there are too many possible inferences to predict, stick to the main theme (cooking food may be responsible for our bodies evolving) and use Content Clues to do any necessary research.

Step 5: Evaluate the Answer Choices
(E) is correct. While the authors spend a lot of time presenting evidence and pushing the idea that we've adapted to our cooked-food diet, they concede in the last paragraph that other possible explanations exist and further testing is warranted.

(A) is Out of Scope. The authors never discuss the relative health benefits of raw versus cooked food.

(B) is a Distortion. The suggestion is that people evolved *because* they started eating cooked food, not that they had to evolve first before eating cooked food.

(C) is not supported. By lines 38–41, human ancestors may have started cooking food about 1.9 million years ago, and the earliest date mentioned in the paragraph about using fire was only 250,000 years ago (lines 19–22).

(D) is a Distortion. A sedentary lifestyle is mentioned in line 9, and at that point it's mentioned as the rare circumstance in which people could live on raw food instead of cooked food. There's no indication that humans had to start leading sedentary lives to eat cooked food.

24. (E) Global

Step 2: Identify the Question Type
The question asks for a description of the "structure of the passage" as a whole, making this a Global question.

Step 3: Research the Relevant Text
Because the question asks about the entire passage, all of the text is relevant. Use the margin notes for the passage to get a sense of the structure.

Step 4: Make a Prediction
The main point of the passage occurs in the first paragraph. Once that paragraph lays down the main idea, the remaining paragraphs expand on that idea and provide additional evidence about what it all means.

Step 5: Evaluate the Answer Choices
(E) is correct. The major claim is in the first paragraph, and the second and third paragraphs expand on that claim and explore its implications.

(A) is a Distortion. The authors don't make any predictions. And the third paragraph doesn't disconfirm anything; it merely explains why there's still need for more testing.

(B) is a Distortion. The second paragraph expands upon the theory from the first paragraph; it doesn't introduce an alternative theory. And the third paragraph suggests that further testing is needed, but it does not describe what that testing would entail.

(C) is a Distortion. Any alternative to the cooked-food theory doesn't come up until the third paragraph, in which it's claimed that a high raw-meat diet could explain our current digestive anatomy. However, that's just an alternative, traditional idea, not an objection to the authors' cooked-food theory.

(D) is a Distortion. The authors only offer one proposal in the first paragraph: that cooked-food diets are responsible for our anatomical evolutionary changes.

25. (B) Logic Reasoning (Strengthen)

Step 2: Identify the Question Type
The question asks for something that would "provide the most support" for a claim in the passage. That makes this a Strengthen question, like the ones found in Logical Reasoning.

Step 3: Research the Relevant Text
The question refers to the authors' claim immediately before the parenthetical in the first paragraph. The parenthetical is in lines 19–22, so the claim being questioned is the one in lines 16–19.

Step 4: Make a Prediction
The point being argued in lines 16–19 is that people are wrong to assume that cooking started too recently to impact our evolution. In other words, the authors are arguing that cooking food *could* have impacted our evolution. As evidence, the authors offer the information about fire and "earth ovens" being used 250,000 years ago. However, the authors assume that 250,000 years is sufficient time for biological adaptations to occur. If it takes a million years or more to adapt, then 250,000-year-old ovens aren't going to be very convincing. To strengthen their argument, the authors would need further evidence showing that 250,000 years is enough time for people to adapt.

Step 5: Evaluate the Answer Choices
(B) is correct. If it took only 5,000 years for humans to adapt to drinking milk, then 250,000 years should be more than enough time to adapt to eating cooked food.

(A) is irrelevant. How humans cut up animals has no bearing on whether cooking the food impacted our biological evolution.

(C) is a 180, at worst. Saying that early uses of fire and earth ovens coincided with ice ages could suggest that the fires were used for warmth, not cooking. If the 250,000-year-old fires weren't used for cooking, then that offers no help to the authors' claims.

(D) is irrelevant. The argument is not about what types of food people ate (plants versus meat). It's about whether that food was cooked or not, and whether that impacted our biological evolution. This choice does not address that argument.

(E) is Out of Scope. This pulls the tooth and jaw details from the second paragraph, and adds in information about brain volume. However, this does nothing to support whether or not any of these changes were due to humans cooking food.

26. (D) Inference

Step 2: Identify the Question Type
The question asks for something the authors *suggest*, making this an Inference question.

Step 3: Research the Relevant Text
The question refers to the second paragraph, so use the margin notes as a basis for checking the answer choices.

Step 4: Make a Prediction
The second paragraph is mostly about tooth and jaw evidence. There's information about them shrinking 100,000 years ago, and the authors suggest that cooking food is at

least partially responsible for that. Start with that, and use clues in the answer choices to test answers as needed.

Step 5: Evaluate the Answer Choices

(D) is supported in lines 35–38, which claim that dental reduction varied depending partially on "when improvements in cooking technology were adopted."

(A) is Extreme. In lines 38–41, it's suggested that teeth and jaws could have reduced in size about 1.9 million years ago, not *only* during the period 100,000 years ago.

(B) is a Distortion. It's not that humans can't survive on a high-meat diet, it's that they're unlikely to do well on a high *raw* meat diet. We're fine if the meat is cooked.

(C) is not supported, and is a Faulty Use of Detail. It's the third paragraph, not the second, in which the authors suggest that it's difficult to reconstruct the evolution of certain digestive system parts. Besides, that difficulty doesn't mean it's not well understood.

(E) is a 180. In lines 35–38, it's said there was variation in when cooking technology was adopted in different regions. They didn't all change at the same time.

27. (D) Global

Step 2: Identify the Question Type

The question asks for the "primary purpose" of the entire passage, making this a Global question.

Step 3: Research the Relevant Text

As with any Global question, the entire text is relevant. Instead of going back into the passage, refer to the Purpose as predicted while reading the passage.

Step 4: Make a Prediction

The authors' purpose was informative, providing evidence to support their theory about cooked food impacting our evolution.

Step 5: Evaluate the Answer Choices

(D) is correct, as the authors propose the hypothesis that cooked food impacted our evolution, and they provide evidence to support that hypothesis.

(A) is a Distortion. The biological evolution of humans is never presented as a puzzle or something that needs to be solved.

(B) is a Distortion. The authors do identify a potential misconception at the beginning, but the purpose of the passage is to correct that misconception and offer the new theory about cooked food impacting human evolution.

(C) is a Distortion. The authors present a hypothesis and provide details about it, but they're not trying to clarify what it means. They're just presenting it as is.

(E) is a Distortion. The authors provide evidence in support of their own theory. They're not trying to undermine any other theory or principle.

Section II: Logical Reasoning

Q#	Question Type	Correct	Difficulty
1	Flaw	B	★
2	Assumption (Necessary)	A	★
3	Point at Issue (Agree)	B	★
4	Flaw	A	★
5	Principle (Identify/Strengthen)	D	★★
6	Inference	E	★★
7	Strengthen	D	★★
8	Role of a Statement	B	★
9	Weaken	C	★★
10	Inference	E	★★
11	Weaken	C	★
12	Assumption (Necessary)	D	★
13	Strengthen (EXCEPT)	A	★★
14	Assumption (Sufficient)	D	★★★
15	Main Point	A	★
16	Principle (Identify/Strengthen)	B	★
17	Flaw	E	★
18	Inference	B	★
19	Parallel Flaw	B	★★★
20	Inference	A	★★
21	Assumption (Necessary)	B	★★★
22	Parallel Reasoning	D	★★★★
23	Role of a Statement	C	★★★★
24	Inference	E	★★★
25	Paradox	C	★★

1. (B) Flaw

Step 1: Identify the Question Type
The correct answer will describe what is *flawed* about the philosopher's reasoning, making this a Flaw question.

Step 2: Untangle the Stimulus
The philosopher argues against people who claim that university students are not interested in philosophical issues. In other words, the philosopher concludes that students *are* interested in philosophical issues. As evidence, the philosopher cites the deep interest in philosophy shown by students who attend his talks.

Step 3: Make a Prediction
Of course those students are going to be interested in philosophy. They're the ones attending talks on philosophy. But what about all of the students who *don't* attend those talks? The philosopher assumes that most students will have the same interest in philosophy as those who attend the talks. This is a commonly tested flaw of drawing a conclusion about a large group of people based on a sample that may not be representative. You would think a philosopher would know better!

Step 4: Evaluate the Answer Choices
(B) accurately describes the representative error made by the philosopher.

(A) is not accurate. The word *interest* never changes meaning. It always refers to a desire to learn more about something.

(C) is Out of Scope. The philosopher is not trying to draw a conclusion about the *worth* of philosophy. Instead, the philosopher is trying to draw a conclusion about people's interest in philosophy.

(D) is a Distortion. The argument is about whether there's interest in philosophy or not. There's no discussion of whether that interest is increasing or decreasing.

(E) is Out of Scope. The philosopher makes no judgment about whether student interest is good or not. The argument is solely about whether such interest exists.

2. (A) Assumption (Necessary)

Step 1: Identify the Question Type
The question asks for an *assumption* that the argument *requires*, making this a Necessary Assumption question.

Step 2: Untangle the Stimulus
In an ancient settlement, an engraved fossil was found depicting a mammoth. The author uses this fossil as evidence to conclude that the settlement was occupied when mammoths roamed the area.

Step 3: Make a Prediction
Just because the engraved fossil was found at the settlement doesn't mean it was engraved there. Perhaps it was engraved hundreds or even thousands of years earlier and then passed down to the settlement long after the mammoths disappeared. Or perhaps, the settlement's inhabitants just liked carving mammoths even though there none around for them to see. For this argument to work, the author must assume that the engraving was made, and the mammoths still existed, when the settlement was around.

Step 4: Evaluate the Answer Choices
(A) matches the prediction. Note that **(A)** is not sufficient to guarantee that mammoths lived in the area, but it is necessary for the author to use the engraving as evidence that the settlement was occupied when mammoths were around. Put to the Denial Test, **(A)** would read "the engraving was *not* made when the settlement was occupied." In that case, the author's argument would fall apart because it disassociates the engraving's creation from the settlement's occupation.

(B) is not necessary. The fossil itself doesn't have to be a mammoth bone. All that matters is that the engraving depicted a mammoth, suggesting they were still around.

(C) is irrelevant. The author is arguing that mammoths were still in the area when the settlement was occupied. What happened when the mammoths died off in the area, or whether other mammoths existed elsewhere, has no bearing on the argument.

(D) is not necessary. It doesn't matter if the technique was unique or not. Even if the technique was used elsewhere, it still depicted a mammoth and could be evidence of mammoths in the area at the time of the settlement.

(E) is Extreme. Even if there were a scientific way of dating the fossil bone, it could still verify the author's conclusion. The author's argument does not rely on the lack of scientific verification.

3. (B) Point at Issue (Agree)

Step 1: Identify the Question Type
The question is asking for something based on a dialogue between two speakers. This is usually the sign of a Point at Issue question, and that is true here. However, unlike most Point at Issue questions, this one asks for something about which both speakers *agree* rather than disagree. When the LSAT deviates from the norm, it pays to take your time and read carefully.

Step 2: Untangle the Stimulus
Durham argues that the mayor will agree to increasing taxes. The evidence is that the mayor must do so to get her top-priority road repair proposal accepted by city council. Espinoza argues that avoiding a tax increase is actually more important than the proposal, and thus concludes that the proposal will be rejected.

Step 3: Make a Prediction

There's a lot more disagreement than agreement here. However, both speakers recognize a connection between the mayor's willingness to increase taxes and the likelihood of her proposal getting accepted by city council. Durham claims that a willingness to increase taxes is necessary to get the proposal accepted, and Espinoza suggests that not increasing taxes is going to prevent the proposal from being accepted—which means the tax increase is necessary, just as Durham claims. That's the point of agreement.

Step 4: Evaluate the Answer Choices

(B) is correct, describing both authors' suggestion that the mayor's agreement to a tax increase is necessary to getting her proposal accepted.

(A) is a 180. Durham says she will agree to increased taxes, but Espinoza suggests she won't because it's more important to avoid doing that.

(C) is a 180. Durham says the proposal is her top priority, while Espinoza argues that avoiding a tax increase is more important.

(D) is also a 180. Espinoza argues that the proposal will not pass. However, Durham is arguing that the mayor is doing what she needs, suggesting that the proposal may indeed pass.

(E) is another 180. Espinoza claims that avoiding a tax increase is more important. However, Durham argues that she'd rather agree to a tax increase because the road repair proposal is her top priority.

4. (A) Flaw

Step 1: Identify the Question Type

The question asks why the given argument is "vulnerable to criticism." That's common language indicating a Flaw question.

Step 2: Untangle the Stimulus

Unlike politicians, who attack opposing arguments by making them sound terrible, scholars actually make opposing arguments sound great. By doing so, the scholars' colleagues are more impressed and are more likely to be convinced by the scholars' arguments. From that, the author argues that politicians could be more persuasive if they acted more like the scholars.

Step 3: Make a Prediction

The problem is that the scholars' approach works great with their professional colleagues. However, what works for one group doesn't necessarily work for everyone. Voters, in general, may not respond to the "praise-the-opponent" approach in the same way professional scholars do. The author is assuming that the approach will be equally effective

in different scenarios, and the correct answer will point out how that is not necessarily the case.

Step 4: Evaluate the Answer Choices

(A) is a match.

(B) is irrelevant. It doesn't matter whether it's easy or difficult to find good things to say. If it's going to be a more productive approach, then it can still be worth the effort.

(C) is a Distortion. The author does describe two different argumentative styles. However, it makes no difference if they could both be used for two similar audiences. The author is suggesting that only one be used for two *different* audiences.

(D) may be accurate, but it does not make the argument invalid. Even if persuasion wasn't a chief aim for one group (e.g., the scholars may not really care about persuading others), the argument wouldn't change. And the argument would still be invalid for equating two different scenarios that are not necessarily the same.

(E) is not supported. There is no suggestion that politicians will attack opponents for positions on which they agree. The author could very well assume that politicians only attack positions on which they disagree, and the argument would be the same—and still flawed.

5. (D) Principle (Identify/Strengthen)

Step 1: Identify the Question Type

The question directly asks for a principle, and one that "helps to justify" the given argument. That makes this an Identify the Principle question that will work like a Strengthen question.

Step 2: Untangle the Stimulus

The first couple of sentences provide a lot of details and background information. However, the core of the argument is the last sentence. The lawyer argues that doctors can be guilty of manslaughter if they intentionally stop a person's life and are unable to revive that person.

Step 3: Make a Prediction

Specifically, the lawyer is charging doctors with manslaughter if they cannot resuscitate a person whose life they intentionally stopped—even for the sake of surgery. To justify this accusation, a principle will conform to this logic but be a little broader in scope: anyone who cannot resuscitate a person after intentionally stopping that person's life is guilty of manslaughter.

Step 4: Evaluate the Answer Choices

(D) is correct, effectively making the medical team guilty of manslaughter if they cease a person's life and that cessation is permanent (i.e., they cannot revive the person).

(A) is not strong enough. This may seem like an Extreme answer, as the lawyer is not saying manslaughter is warranted for *any* medical procedure that could result in death—only those in which doctors *deliberately* stop the patient's life.

However, principles are meant to be broader to apply to other circumstances as well. The real problem here is that, even if this principle were true, it only says that the medical team *could* be charged with manslaughter. That is not enough to justify the lawyer's claim that the medical team *would* absolutely be guilty.

(B) is a Distortion. This makes the patient dying a necessary condition for manslaughter (i.e., the doctors *can* be guilty of manslaughter only if the patient dies). However, by that logic, a patient dying does not guarantee it being manslaughter. So that is not enough to justify the lawyer's position, which claims that the patient dying *is* sufficient to guarantee a manslaughter accusation.

(C) is a Distortion. This suggests that, in order to be charged with manslaughter, the intention must be to *irreversibly* stop a person's live. However, the doctor's intention is not to make the loss of life irreversible. The intention is to stop life temporarily and revive the person later.

(E) is a 180. This suggests that patient consent, which must be gained for the surgeries in question, could actually invalidate the accusation of manslaughter.

6. (E) Inference

Step 1: Identify the Question Type
The correct answer "must be true" based on the statements given, making this an Inference question.

Step 2: Untangle the Stimulus
The professor presents several pieces of Formal Logic. First, to accurately judge the greatness of literary works, one needs specialized training.

If	judge greatness	→	specialized training

That training is also necessary for being a literary professor.

If	literary professor	→	specialized training

The final claim is that most readers don't have that necessary training.

If	part of the vast majority of the reading public	→	~ specialized training

Step 3: Make a Prediction
The third statement can be combined with the contrapositive of the first: Because most readers don't have the necessary

training, they cannot accurately judge the greatness of literary works. Likewise, the third statement can be combined with the contrapositive of the second: that same lack of necessary training means that most readers cannot be literary professors. The correct answer is likely to draw at least one, if not both, of these Formal Logic–based conclusions.

Step 4: Evaluate the Answer Choices
(E) is correct. Accurate judgment requires specialized training. Because most readers don't have that training, it can be deduced (via contrapositive) that they can't accurately judge.

(A) is not necessarily true. By the second claim, because John's professor is a literary professor, she must have the necessary specialized training. However, by the first claim, having that training is still only necessary for judging works of literature accurately. It is not sufficient, and is thus not a guarantee that she's able to do so.

(B) is not necessarily true. The specialized training is necessary for being a literary professor, but it could be necessary for other jobs, too. So, even if one is not a literary professor, one could still receive that training and thus have what's necessary to accurately judge works of literature.

(C) is Out of Scope. The last claim only states that most readers don't have access to the training, but there is no suggestion that those people *should* have access to it.

(D) is not necessarily true. It is only said that the *majority* of the reading public does not have access to the training. However, there could still be plenty of readers who *do* have access to that training, and that very well could include literature professors.

7. (D) Strengthen

Step 1: Identify the Question Type
The question asks for something that "helps to justify" a position, making this a Strengthen question. Unlike most Strengthen questions, the correct answer here will merely support a *contention* rather than an entire argument. That suggests the advocates will not have much evidence, if any. The correct answer will provide some much-needed evidence.

Step 2: Untangle the Stimulus
The advocates' contention is in the last sentence. They claim that geothermic power plants will soon provide power to most areas of the world. As expected, the advocates provide no evidence for that claim. However, it's interesting to note that the background info (which provides a lot of science-based details about geothermic power) mentions that the reservoirs needed for geothermic power plants can currently only be reached in limited areas of the world.

Step 3: Make a Prediction
In a sense, this question works a lot like a Paradox question. It presents an interesting mystery: If geothermic power plants

are only available in limited parts of the world, why do the advocates feel that most areas will soon get geothermic power? They must assume something is going to change, and the correct answer should provide evidence that validates that assumption.

Step 4: Evaluate the Answer Choices

(D) is correct. This suggests a change is coming, and technology may allow us to soon dig deeper and find the reservoirs needed to create more geothermal power plants, as the advocates conclude.

(A) is irrelevant. This offers a reason why geothermal power plants would be preferable, but it offers no support for the claim that such plants will become more available in the near future.

(B) is also irrelevant. Even if geothermal power plants produce as much energy as traditional power plants, they're still only available in limited areas of the world. There's no evidence that they will become more worldwide in the near future.

(C) is a 180. This gives a reason why geothermal power plants may *not* be built, running counter to the advocates' claim.

(E) is irrelevant. If almost all power plants become more cost-efficient, then that gives no extra advantage to geothermal plants, providing no support for why they will become more prevalent in the near future.

8. (B) Role of a Statement

Step 1: Identify the Question Type

The question stem presents a claim from the stimulus and asks for its "role in the argument," making this a Role of a Statement question.

Step 2: Untangle the Stimulus

The claim in question (that one should not confuse a desire for money with a desire for material goods) is the very first sentence. And the Keyword *should* indicates a recommendation, which is often an author's conclusion. And that is the case here, as the remaining sentences provide evidence of the difference between money (which can buy non-material goods) and material goods (which can provide non-monetary value).

Step 3: Make a Prediction

The claim in question is the author's conclusion, supported by the evidence in the final two sentences.

Step 4: Evaluate the Answer Choices

(B) is correct.

(A) is a Distortion. The first claim is a generalization. However, the examples are provided to support the opening sentence, not the other way around.

(C) is not accurate. There is no other conclusion other than the first sentence. And everything else supports the first sentence, not the other way around.

(D) is Half-Right/Half-Wrong. The first sentence is absolutely a recommendation. However, the examples in the evidence are all consistent with that recommendation, not counter to it.

(E) is a Distortion. There is no problem to be solved. Besides, the first sentence does not provide a basis for the conclusion. It *is* the conclusion.

9. (C) Weaken

Step 1: Identify the Question Type

The question asks for something that *undermines* the given argument, which is a common term to indicate a Weaken question.

Step 2: Untangle the Stimulus

Yu is contradicting the menu at Jason's Restaurant, implying that some of the restaurant's food *is* grown with pesticides. The evidence is that Jason's Restaurant buys produce at Kelly's Grocery, and Yu saw produce delivered to Kelly's from MegaFarm, which uses pesticides on *all* its crops.

Step 3: Make a Prediction

Yu provides evidence that Jason's Restaurant buys produce from a store that sells produce grown with pesticides. However, that doesn't mean that the store *only* sells produce with pesticides. Yu overlooks the possibility that Kelly's also sells produce *not* grown with pesticides, and Jason only purchases that produce. The correct answer will exploit this error and show how Jason could still buy at Kelly's and still correctly advertise a no-pesticide policy.

Step 4: Evaluate the Answer Choices

(C) is correct. This suggests that even if Kelly's carries pesticide-grown produce (from MegaFarm), they still sell produce not grown with pesticides, and Jason can identify that produce clearly without buying the pesticide-covered produce.

(A) is irrelevant. Even if Jason was ignorant of the source of Kelly's produce, the produce he purchases would still be grown with pesticides, and Yu would still have a valid argument.

(B) is irrelevant. Even if Jason also buys from other locations that don't use pesticides, he still purchases from Kelly's, which *does* have produce grown with pesticides. Yu's argument still stands.

(D) is Out of Scope. The argument is not about safety. It's about whether or not pesticides are used. Even if they're government approved, they're still being used, and Jason is still buying food grown with them, as Yu argues.

(E) is irrelevant. It doesn't matter what *most* of Kelly's customers would do; it only matters what Jason would do.

Besides, even if he didn't *know* he was buying produce grown with pesticides, he still could be buying it. And that's enough to support, not counter, Yu's argument.

10. (E) Inference

Step 1: Identify the Question Type
The correct answer to this question will fill in the blank at the end of the stimulus. That blank is preceded by [*t*]*herefore*, which means everything else will provide support for what fills in that blank. That makes this an Inference question.

Step 2: Untangle the Stimulus
The author is discussing song overlapping, which is when one bird is singing and another bird cuts in and starts singing a different song at the same time. (How rude!) Some studies claim this is aggressive behavior. However, the author argues that these studies are based on birds' responses, and any response can be considered a reaction to aggressive behavior.

Step 3: Make a Prediction
The author seems skeptical. If people can say *any* response (even no response) is a reaction to aggressive behavior, then it stands to reason that *any* behavior could be perceived as aggressive—even behavior that is *not* actually aggressive. That means that, perhaps, the studies aren't exactly conclusive. And that is likely the conclusion that will fill in the blank.

For this question, it is important not to commit a reasoning flaw that the LSAT often tests: Insufficient evidence does not disprove an argument. In other words, just because the evidence of bird responses is not enough to label the behavior aggressive, that doesn't mean the behavior is absolutely *not* aggressive. There just needs to be more and/or better evidence to make that claim. The correct answer needs to be qualified and not absolutely deny the possibility of aggressive behavior.

Step 4: Evaluate the Answer Choices
(E) is correct, adequately summarizing the author's skepticism without taking it too far.

(A) is a Distortion. It's not about the responses being unpredictable. The author is suggesting that the behavior may not actually be aggressive.

(B) is Extreme. While the tests in the studies are not good enough to warrant a claim of aggressive behavior, that's not to say such tests provide *no* insight whatsoever.

(C) is a Distortion. The author is not saying that the studies are wrong. The author is merely suggesting that the evidence is not good enough to warrant that conclusion. The author may agree with the studies, but just wants better evidence to support them.

(D) is Extreme and Out of Scope. The argument is about whether or not song overlapping is aggressive, not whether or not it is communicative. Besides, the author only suggests that song overlapping *may* not be aggressive. The author never outright denies any particular function.

11. (C) Weaken

Step 1: Identify the Question Type
The question asks for something that "most weakens the argument," making this a Weaken question.

Step 2: Untangle the Stimulus
The author presents information showing how people find excessive blinking to be a sign of poor performance in a political debate. The author concludes that this can have a negative impact on election results. The evidence is that blinking does not affect political performance. Other factors, such as knowledge and confidence, are surely more important.

Step 3: Make a Prediction
To suggest that this can harm election results, the author must assume that good candidates can be dismissed when judged for excessively blinking. However, if those heavy blinkers are actually poor candidates, then the author's argument is invalid; judgments based on blinking might instead be valuable. The correct answer will show how focusing on blinking can have a positive impact, contrary to what the author suggests.

Step 4: Evaluate the Answer Choices
(C) is correct. The author argues that confidence contributes to political performance. If excessive blinking indicates a lack of confidence, then blinking could be a sign of problems to come. That would make it good for voters to notice, not deleterious (harmful), as the author claims.

(A) is not strong enough. The author's conclusion is that any impact is sure to be bad. That doesn't mean there's always an impact. It's just always bad when there is an impact. So, even if voters' judgments are rarely a factor, they could still always be harmful when they *do* affect results, and the author's argument would still stand.

(B) is an Irrelevant Comparison. It doesn't matter whether the effect of seeing infrequent blinking is the same as or different from the effect of seeing excessive blinking. The author's argument is about whether or not election results will be harmed, and this has no bearing on that argument.

(D) is irrelevant. A connection between knowledge and confidence has nothing to do with whether blinking has any potential impact on election results.

(E) is irrelevant. Although knowledge is a better indicator of a candidate's potential performance, this does nothing to impact the author's argument about whether or not using blinking as a judgment is harmful.

12. (D) Assumption (Necessary)

Step 1: Identify the Question Type
The question asks for an "assumption required," making this a Necessary Assumption question.

Step 2: Untangle the Stimulus
The scientist concludes that some pundits are wrong: The public is *not* afraid of scientists. As evidence, the scientist claims to have never met anyone, throughout several decades, who was afraid of scientists.

Step 3: Make a Prediction
The scientist treats personal experience as indicative of the truth of people in general. In other words, the scientist assumes that, just because *she* has never met anyone afraid of scientists, people in general must not have that fear. Furthermore, she also assumes that if she *did* meet people who were fearful of scientists, she would be able to notice/sense that fear.

Step 4: Evaluate the Answer Choices
(D) is correct. In Formal Logic terms, the scientist is assuming: If I've never met someone afraid of scientists, then the general public couldn't possibly fear scientists. This answer choice just presents the contrapositive: If the public *did* fear scientists, I would have met *somebody* who is afraid of scientists.

(A) is Out of Scope and, if anything, a 180. This brings up manipulation and being on guard, which have no direct connection to anything in the argument. Worse yet, this suggests there might be good reason for people to be concerned about science and/or scientists, contrary to the scientist's argument.

(B) is Out of Scope. This raises the condition of understanding science, which has no connection to anything in the argument. Besides, by this logic, people *could* still fear scientists if they didn't understand science, and that would be contrary to the scientist's argument.

(C) is Out of Scope. The argument is only about whether people fear scientists. Whether or not they are further concerned about technology is irrelevant to the argument at hand.

(E) is Out of Scope. The scientist has never met anybody who claims to be afraid of scientists. So, how such hypothetical people actually feel is irrelevant.

13. (A) Strengthen (EXCEPT)

Step 1: Identify the Question Type
The question is asking for information that *strengthens* the given argument, making this a Strengthen question. However,

it's important to pay attention to the EXCEPT, which means it's the incorrect choices that will strengthen the argument. The correct answer will be the one that does not strengthen the argument; it will either weaken the argument or have no effect.

Step 2: Untangle the Stimulus
The scientist is arguing against traditional thinking by concluding that the earliest flying dinosaurs merely glided from trees rather than taking off from the ground. The evidence is that gliding can be done with wings that are simpler than those usually associated with flying dinosaurs.

Step 3: Make a Prediction
The evidence here is fairly scant. While gliding can be done with simple wings, the scientist overlooks the possibility that dinosaurs could still use those same wings to take flight from the ground. Also, in order to glide from trees, the scientist must assume that those early dinosaurs were able to get up in the trees in the first place. The scientist could use a lot of help here. A choice will strengthen the argument if it suggests that the dinosaurs didn't take off from the ground or that they spent time in the trees. The correct answer will show the opposite or be completely irrelevant.

Step 4: Evaluate the Answer Choices
(A) is correct, as it doesn't help the scientist at all. If early dinosaurs built nests at the base of trees, that suggests they may have been unable to climb trees. In that case, they wouldn't have glided from the trees.

(B) strengthens the argument. This suggests they were able to climb trees, which would put them in a good position from which they could glide, as the scientist argues.

(C) strengthens the argument. This suggests the early dinosaurs' simple wings were good for gliding and not so great for taking flight. That definitely supports the scientist's pro-gliding stance.

(D) strengthens the argument. This suggests that early dinosaurs would have had trouble running, which would make it difficult to get the running start for taking flight. That makes gliding a more likely option.

(E) strengthens the argument, suggesting the early dinosaurs had a reason to climb trees—to get away from predators. And once in the trees, the dinosaurs would have been in a good position to glide.

14. (D) Assumption (Sufficient)

Step 1: Identify the Question Type
The correct answer, "if [it] is assumed," will logically complete the argument. That makes this a Sufficient Assumption question.

Step 2: Untangle the Stimulus

The author concludes (*it follows*) that critics are mistaken: Not all legitimate art has a concern for beauty. The evidence is that some legitimate art can arouse anger, and all such art calls for intervention in the world.

Step 3: Make a Prediction

As is typical with Sufficient Assumption questions, this argument hinges on Mismatched Concepts. By the evidence, it can be deduced that some legitimate art calls for intervention. However, the conclusion suddenly brings up concern for beauty, which is not logically connected to anything in the evidence. The author assumes a connection, namely that art that calls for intervention is not concerned with beauty.

Step 4: Evaluate the Answer Choices

(D) matches the prediction.

(A) is Out of Scope. The conclusion is only about legitimate works of art. The concerns of non-legitimate art are irrelevant to the argument.

(B) is a 180. This claims that all legitimate art must be concerned exclusively with beauty, which is the complete opposite of the what the author concludes.

(C) is a Distortion. The author's conclusion is that some legitimate art is *not* concerned with beauty. If beauty were only a secondary concern, as this choice suggests, it would still be a concern. That would not be consistent with the author's conclusion.

(E) is a Distortion. The author claims that all legitimate art that arouses anger will call for intervention. However, that's not to say that *only* such art is legitimate. There could be plenty of other legitimate artwork. Besides, this has nothing to do with the concern for beauty, which is the real missing piece of the puzzle.

15. (A) Main Point

Step 1: Identify the Question Type

The question asks for the "overall conclusion" of the argument, making this a Main Point question.

Step 2: Untangle the Stimulus

The Keyword *clearly* in the first sentence is a strong indicator of a conclusion. In that sentence, the author argues that children understand the difference between real and pretend. Sure enough, the remaining sentences provide the evidence for that claim: Kids can correctly identify the difference once they learn to speak. They realize that their silly dads aren't actually lions. And, without such understanding, it would be impossible to explain why kids love make-believe.

Step 3: Make a Prediction

Everything after the first sentence is merely evidence to support that opening claim: Kids understand the difference between real and pretend. That's the main point.

Step 4: Evaluate the Answer Choices

(A) is correct.

(B) is evidence for the author's claim, not the conclusion itself.

(C) is evidence that supports the author's claim, not the conclusion itself.

(D) is part of the evidence, not the author's conclusion.

(E) is evidence, not a conclusion. Because of this fact given at the end of the stimulus, the author believes that children do, in fact, know the difference. It's *that* belief that is the overall conclusion.

16. (B) Principle (Identify/Strengthen)

Step 1: Identify the Question Type

The question directly asks for a principle, and one that would "help to justify" the given argument. That makes this an Identify the Principle question that utilizes the skills of a Strengthen question.

Step 2: Untangle the Stimulus

The minister concludes ([*t*]*herefore*) that his country should not sign an international pollution agreement. The evidence is that, although the agreement would reduce pollution, it would also reduce economic growth in the minister's countries as well as others.

Step 3: Make a Prediction

The refusal to take an environmental stance is made based on economic grounds. That suggests that the minister is acting on the principle that economic concerns are more important than environmental ones. The correct answer should confirm that principle.

Step 4: Evaluate the Answer Choices

(B) is correct.

(A) is a 180. The environment minister suggests that the agreement *would* achieve its stated goals.

(C) is Out of Scope. The environment minister never mentions or suggests any better means of reducing ocean pollution.

(D) is not enough to justify the conclusion. While the minister does consider both his own country's and other countries' economies, this offers no reason for why that consideration outweighs the benefits of the pollution agreement.

(E) is a Distortion. This would justify signing an agreement that would *not* reduce economic growth. However, that's not the same as justifying *not* signing an agreement that *will* reduce growth.

17. (E) Flaw

Step 1: Identify the Question Type
The correct answer will describe why the given argument is *flawed*, making this a Flaw question.

Step 2: Untangle the Stimulus
The advocate concludes ([t]*herefore*) that taking cold medicine is counterproductive. The evidence is that cold sufferers who reported taking cold medicine also reported more severe symptoms than did cold sufferers who did not take any medicine.

Step 3: Make a Prediction
By saying cold medicine is counterproductive, the advocate is implying that the cold medicine *caused* sufferers to experience more severe symptoms. As with most causal arguments, this one overlooks three commonly tested possibilities: 1) There could be an alternative explanation (i.e., it wasn't the cold medicine but something else that caused the bad symptoms). 2) The advocate could have the causality reversed (i.e., the presence of severe symptoms is what caused people to take cold medicine, not the other way around). 3) It could all be a coincidence (i.e., the medicine has nothing to do with symptoms). The correct answer will point out any one of these overlooked possibilities.

Step 4: Evaluate the Answer Choices
(E) is correct, suggesting the advocate has the causality reversed. Those severe symptoms could be the cause of people taking the medicine, not a side effect of the medicine.

(A) is Out of Scope. The advocate's conclusion is based on what people reported experiencing, not what people believe.

(B) is Out of Scope. The people in the study are just said to be those who recovered from colds. There is no claim or implication of them being treated as experts.

(C) is Out of Scope. There is nothing that is said to happen in *most* cases. And the advocate is making a general claim, not a conclusion about just one case.

(D) describes the flaw of necessity versus sufficiency. However, there are no conditional statements or Formal Logic, so nothing is presented as necessary or sufficient.

18. (B) Inference

Step 1: Identify the Question Type
The correct answer will fill in the blank at the end of the stimulus. That blank concludes a line of thought, so it will be supported by the information that precedes it. That makes this an Inference question.

Step 2: Untangle the Stimulus
The author begins by describing two groups of people: those who avoid unpleasant truths and dislike confrontation, and those who prefer to hear the truth no matter what. The author uses this to set up a hypothetical claim: What if people in the first group (those who avoid unpleasant truths) treated others the way they like to be treated?

Step 3: Make a Prediction
If the first group treated everybody the way they like to be treated, then they would avoid telling others unpleasant truths. All of that unpleasantness would be withheld, and confrontation would be avoided. That would suit them just fine. However, this is completely opposite of what the second group of folks want, which is pure openness: nothing gets withheld. So, if the first group just did things their own way, it's logical to deduce that such actions would disappoint people in the second group.

Step 4: Evaluate the Answer Choices
(B) matches the predication and is correct.

(A) is not supported. The hypothetical situation has the people in the first group treating others consistently with their own desires. So, they will act as they normally do, not in a way that is different from normal.

(C) is not supported. The principle of behavior is to treat others as you would want them to treat you. If people in the first group treated everybody this way (by withholding unpleasant truths), the people in the second group may still treat people differently (they'd speak the truth no matter what). However, the second group could still be acting on the same *principle*: Treat others the way you want to be treated. It's the specific behavior that's different, not the principle.

(D) is not supported. If the first group acts one way, the people in the second group could still respond in the way *they* prefer: by telling the truth no matter what.

(E) is a 180. The second group doesn't like to avoid the truth, so they would not approve of the first group's behavior.

19. (B) Parallel Flaw

Step 1: Identify the Question Type
The correct answer will provide "flawed reasoning" that is "most closely parallel" to the reasoning in the stimulus. That makes this a Parallel Flaw question.

Step 2: Untangle the Stimulus
The given argument is based on Formal Logic, which means it's highly likely that the flaw will be a confusion of necessary and sufficient conditions. The first two claims offer two pieces of Formal Logic, both of which produce the same result: 1) If you study history, you'll appreciate differences among civilizations, and 2) If you reflect on your own civilization, you'll appreciate differences among civilizations.

If	study history	→	appreciate differences

If	reflect on own civilization	→	appreciate differences

The author uses this to draw a Formal Logic conclusion: If you study history, you will reflect on your own civilization.

If	study history	→	reflect on own civilization

Step 3: Make a Prediction

Nice try, author. By the first statement, studying history does guarantee that one appreciates the differences between civilizations. However, while reflecting on one's own civilization could produce the same result, it is not necessary. That would be a backwards application of the logic of the second statement. The correct answer will commit the exact same error. There will be two conditions (studying history and self-reflection) that could produce the same result (appreciate the differences), and the author will erroneously suggest that one condition will bring about the other.

Step 4: Evaluate the Answer Choices

(B) is a match. There are two conditions (learning Latin and studying literature) that can produce the same result (improve vocabulary), and the author suggests that one condition will bring about the other. Learning Latin will improve your vocabulary. However, while studying great literature would have produced the same result, it's not necessary—just as reflecting on one's own civilization wasn't necessary in the original argument.

(A) does not match. There are not two conditions that lead to the same result. Instead, there is a continuous thread of logic.

If	study ancient art	→	appreciate	→	deeper understanding

The same flaw cannot be committed with this string. Further, the conclusion here makes an unwarranted shift from a "deeper understanding" of modern art to a "new appreciation" of modern art, which is unlike anything from the original argument.

(C) does not match. This presents a string of logic instead of two conditions producing the same result.

If	travel	→	appreciation	→	study history

This makes it impossible to commit the same error. So while this argument is flawed (it does treat the final necessary

condition as if it were sufficient), the structure as a whole is not parallel to the original.

(D) does not match. Instead of producing the same result, the two conditions here bring about slightly different results. (Studying helps you *internalize* good habits, and having a positive attitude helps you *retain* those good habits.) And the conclusion brings in an entirely new concept (success in the workplace). The argument may be flawed, but it is structured in a way that is not parallel to the original argument.

(E) does not match. In fact, it's not flawed. The first two claims present a string of logic.

If	read news daily	→	informed	→	appreciate other cultures

The conclusion then presents the logical deduction that the first condition can bring about the last.

20. (A) Inference

Step 1: Identify the Question Type

Accepting the given statements as true, the correct answer "must also be true" based on those statements, making this an Inference question.

Step 2: Untangle the Stimulus

The first two claims describe what happens when you encounter a philosophical paradox. You believe the conclusion is false, but you also believe the evidence is true and thus the conclusion is logical. To solve such a paradox, the author claims one of three actions is required: 1) Accept the conclusion as true, 2) Accept that at least one piece of evidence is false, or 3) Accept that the conclusion is not logical.

Step 3: Make a Prediction

It's interesting to note that the three given requirements directly contradict everything the second sentence claims is our intuition. Thus, it must be true that, one way or another, solving a paradox requires accepting something that contradicts our intuition.

Step 4: Evaluate the Answer Choices

(A) matches the prediction, and is correct.

(B) is a Distortion. By the last claim, there are three ways to solve a philosophical paradox. Two of them are 1) Accept the conclusion as true, and 2) Accept that some of the evidence is false. However, it's still possible to accept the conclusion as false and all of the evidence as true, if we use the third way to solve a paradox: 3) Accept that the conclusion just doesn't follow logically from the evidence.

(C) is an Irrelevant Comparison. No comparison is drawn or suggested based on the number of premises an argument has.

(D) is not supported. The author offers three possible approaches, but it's possible that most people, if not everybody, consistently uses the same one.

(E) is a 180. The author claims that a paradox can be solved using any *one* of the three given techniques. So, even if somebody cannot accept the conclusion as true, there are still two other ways to solve the paradox.

21. (B) Assumption (Necessary)

Step 1: Identify the Question Type
The question asks for an "assumption on which the argument depends," making this a Necessary Assumption question.

Step 2: Untangle the Stimulus
The author concludes ([*t*]*his shows*) that affection plays the same role in both chimp and human communities. The evidence is two-fold: 1) When a chimp shows affection toward others, the other chimps will help protect that chimp, and 2) When a human shows affection toward others, that human will help protect those others.

Step 3: Make a Prediction
The role of affection certainly seems similar. In both communities, it provokes a protective nature. However, the author makes a subtle but significant shift when describing the two communities. In human communities, the one who shows affection is the one who protects others. In the chimp communities, the one who shows affection is protected *by* the other chimps. That's not the same thing. The author assumes a connection between these two events, namely that being protected *by* others is related to providing protection *to* others.

Step 4: Evaluate the Answer Choices
(B) is correct. Using the Denial Test, if affection is not reciprocated, the chimp who feels affection is being protected by others but is not, in turn, providing protection to the others. That would not be the same as what humans do, and the author's argument would be ruined. The author must assume otherwise—that affection is reciprocated, and others feel affection toward the chimp, prompting that chimp to be human-like and protect those others.

(A) is Extreme. The argument is only about affection. It's not about expressing *any* emotion *whenever* one feels that emotion.

(C) is Extreme. Affection does not have to be the *only* emotion that provokes protection. As long as it is just one that does, then chimps and humans can be seen as reacting to affection similarly.

(D) is not necessary. The author need not limit affection to members of a particular group. Even if chimps can feel affectionate toward chimps outside of their social group, the similarity between chimps and humans can still be maintained.

(E) is a Distortion. The defense might appear altruistic. However, it's possible that defending the affectionate group member can be self-serving—protecting that individual to avoid the personal pain of losing that individual. The author never addresses this behavior as altruistic, so it need not be assumed.

22. (D) Parallel Reasoning

Step 1: Identify the Question Type
The question asks for an argument "most similar" to the one in the stimulus. That makes this a Parallel Reasoning question.

Step 2: Untangle the Stimulus
The author concludes (*so*) that the characters of a particular television show will not be made more realistic. The evidence is that doing so will reduce viewership, and the show's writers want to maximize viewership.

Step 3: Make a Prediction
The structure here is based on Formal Logic. If a condition is met (make the characters more realistic), a result would follow (viewership goes down).

If	*more realistic characters*	→	*viewership down*

However, that result is not wanted. So, by contrapositive, the author concludes the condition will not be met.

If	*~ viewership down*	→	*~ more realistic characters*

The correct answer should follow this exact same argument-by-contrapositive approach. As a strategic note, this question does something that Parallel Reasoning questions almost never do. The original argument results in a prediction. However, none of the answer choices provided results in a prediction. Instead, they all conclude something about the past or the present. In a case like this, comparing conclusion types will not be useful, and a more structural comparison (e.g., using Formal Logic) will be necessary.

Step 4: Evaluate the Answer Choices
(D) is a match. It sets up Formal Logic: If the executives were responsible, the losses would have been greater. It then uses the contrapositive to draw the conclusion: The losses were

not greater (they were less), so the executives were *not* responsible.

If	**executives responsible**	→	**losses would have been greater**
If	**losses ~ greater**	→	**executives ~ responsible**

(A) does not match. It does not utilize the contrapositive. Further, the scope shifts a couple of times. The given sufficient condition of the Formal Logic is if the company's failure was *due to* economic collapse. The claim later is that the failure and the collapse just happened at the same time. There is no indication of causality. And the conclusion draws a hesitant conclusion (*probably* not fair), which does not match how the conclusion was drawn in the original argument.

(B) does not match. This is flawed logic, confusing a sufficient condition for a necessary condition. The logic given is: If failure is due to collapse, don't blame the executives. However, it's then given that the failure is *not* due to collapse. That does not mean the logic can be negated and that the executives should be blamed. They may still be free of blame for other reasons.

(C) does not match. It does use a contrapositive. However, it shifts concepts in the conclusion. The Formal Logic is based on a condition of whether or not the executives are *responsible*. The conclusion is about whether you can *blame* the executives. Further, in the original argument, it is given that the necessary result is not wanted (the writers absolutely don't want to shrink their audience). Here, the conclusion is based on a hypothetical situation (*if* you can't say what should have been done differently).

(E) does not match. There is no Formal Logic, and thus nothing with which to form a contrapositive. This just presents a "you can't blame them for the current problems, so you can't praise them for past success" argument, which is not the same as the original.

23. (C) Role of a Statement

Step 1: Identify the Question Type

The question provides a claim and asks for its "role in the argument," making this a Role of a Statement question.

Step 2: Untangle the Stimulus

The author starts with what some people have argued: *T. rex* was so big that it could only scavenge and not hunt. As evidence, it's said that its size would make it too slow to catch its prey. The author then raises an objection (*however*),

claiming that such an argument is too rash. *T. rex*'s prey could have been even slower than *T. rex*.

Step 3: Make a Prediction

The claim in question (*T. rex* could only scavenge and not hunt) is the claim being argued by some people in the first sentence. There is evidence for that claim. However, the author objects to the claim in question, and even addresses the supposed evidence. People might think that *T. rex* was too slow, but the prey could have been even slower. So, the claim in question is something the author objects to, and the author questions it by attacking the evidence provided.

Step 4: Evaluate the Answer Choices

(C) is correct.

(A) is a Distortion. The author's conclusion is that the claim in question is too hasty an argument. That doesn't mean it is wrong or inconsistent with the evidence given. It's just not entirely supported. Saying someone is wrong and saying the conclusion is not properly supported are two different arguments.

(B) is a Distortion. The author calls the claim a "hasty inference" and points out an overlooked possibility. However, the author never actually contends that the claim is actually or probably *false*.

(D) is a Distortion. The claim in question *is* the hypothesis being refuted, not evidence for the hypothesis. Besides, the author never says the hypothesis is false. It's just too hasty an inference and not adequately supported.

(E) is a 180. First off, the claim in question is a conclusion, not evidence. Second, the author's main conclusion is that the claim in question may not be correct. The claim in question and the conclusion are at odds with one another. Neither one is necessary for the other.

24. (E) Inference

Step 1: Identify the Question Type

The question asks for something that can be "properly inferred," making this an Inference question.

Step 2: Untangle the Stimulus

According to the legal theorist, there are only two acceptable theories for sentencing: retributivist (punish the offender) or rehabilitationist (reform the offender). The legal theorist then provides a further requirement for retributivist theories: They must apply the principle that the punishment is proportional to the crime committed. However, the legal theorist claims that one such theory—repeat offenders get longer sentences—violates the principle, as the principle would suggest the same crime always gets the same penalty.

Step 3: Make a Prediction

If the repeat-offender theory violates the proportional punishment principle, then the logic given dictates that it is not an acceptable retributivist theory. That is one major deduction. However, that does *not* mean the theory is entirely unacceptable. According to the first claim, retributivist theories are just *one* acceptable type of theory. Acceptable theories can also be rehabilitationist. So, while the repeat-offender theory is certainly unacceptable as a retributivist theory, it *could* still be overall acceptable if it is relabeled as rehabilitationist.

Step 4: Evaluate the Answer Choices
(E) is correct, summarizing the point that the only way left for the repeat-offender theory to be acceptable is if it's a rehabilitationist theory.

(A) is not supported. It is just said that rehabilitationist theories seek to reform offenders. It never says that punishment cannot be used to bring about that reform.

(B) is not supported. This refers to the repeat-offender theory. However, there is no evidence here that this theory, or any like it, is used as a means of reform.

(C) is Extreme. While labeling the repeat-offender theory as rehabilitationist is the only way left to make it acceptable, it cannot be said that *any* such labeling will guarantee it being acceptable.

(D) is Extreme. Conforming to the proportionality principle is necessary for retributivist theories to be acceptable. However, that doesn't mean *all* such theories will be deemed acceptable.

25. (C) Paradox

Step 1: Identify the Quest ion Type
The question asks for something that "helps to resolve" an "apparent discrepancy," making this a Paradox question.

Step 2: Untangle the Stimulus
The author claims that folktales are studied to help understand the values distinct to individual cultures. *However*, the author claims that different cultures all use the same basic narrative for their folktales, just adapted to the local milieu.

Step 3: Make a Prediction
The mystery here is this: How can people better understand what makes cultural values distinct if they're studying stories that are all based on the same ideas? The author provides a huge hint to the solution. While the stories all use the same narratives, each culture adapts those narratives to its own local environment. The correct answer will likely show how it's those adaptations, and not the shared narratives, that really give insight into the distinct cultural values.

Step 4: Evaluate the Answer Choices
(C) matches the prediction and is correct.

(A) does not help. Even if folktales are the work of an entire culture and not one individual, they are still all based on the same narratives. There's no indication how it's possible to uncover anything distinct.

(B) does not help. Whether folktales are written or oral offers no explanation for how studying them can uncover cultural values.

(D) is, at worst, a 180. This just confirms that folktales need to conform to common themes, which makes it further inexplicable how they're being used to explore values that are distinct.

(E) does not help. While this confirms that folktales can indicate a culture's values, the folktales all still have the same basis. Thus, the values could all still be the same. There's still no explanation how people are able to understand *distinct* values.

Section III: Logical Reasoning

Q#	Question Type	Correct	Difficulty
1	Inference	D	★
2	Paradox	D	★
3	Principle (Identify/Strengthen)	B	★
4	Weaken	A	★
5	Flaw	E	★
6	Strengthen	C	★★★
7	Assumption (Necessary)	C	★★
8	Parallel Flaw	E	★★
9	Flaw	C	★
10	Strengthen	D	★
11	Main Point	A	★
12	Assumption (Sufficient)	E	★★
13	Point at Issue	B	★★★
14	Principle (Identify/Strengthen)	E	★★★
15	Point at Issue	B	★★
16	Flaw	B	★★
17	Paradox	C	★★
18	Assumption (Necessary)	D	★★
19	Weaken	A	★★★★
20	Point at Issue	B	★
21	Strengthen/Weaken (Evaluate the Argument)	D	★★★★
22	Flaw	E	★★★★
23	Parallel Reasoning	E	★★
24	Flaw	D	★★★
25	Principle (Identify/Strengthen)	D	★★

1. (D) Inference

Step 1: Identify the Question Type

The correct answer will fill in the blank at the end of the stimulus. The blank is preceded by the Conclusion Keyword [*h*]*ence*, which means it will be supported by the details before it. That makes this an Inference question.

Step 2: Untangle the Stimulus

The author presents a challenge engineers face in developing self-driving cars: how to avoid problems such as traffic and congestion. It's then noted that fish face similar problems. *However*, fish have developed ways to make those problems less common.

Step 3: Make a Prediction

If fish have found some solutions to problems similar to traffic and congestion, then engineers would probably benefit from knowing some of those solutions. Because fish can't talk, studying how fish navigate would likely be the best way for engineers to learn what fish have learned. That would be the logical conclusion to fill in the blank.

Step 4: Evaluate the Answer Choices

(D) is correct. Note the use of qualified terminology such as "could help," which avoids over-promising on what the author presents.

(A) is a Distortion. While engineers can probably benefit from learning from fish, that's not to say they need to be fish biology experts. Besides, the solution is more about fish behavior than it is fish biology.

(B) is also a Distortion. First, there's no indication that the best drivers are able to minimize driving problems in the way fish minimize their own problems. Further, effective principles for human drivers may be similar to those of fish, but not necessarily exactly the same.

(C) is Extreme. While engineers appear to have potential solutions here by studying fish, that doesn't mean nature will *always* provide guidance with other challenges.

(E) is a Distortion. Perhaps by studying fish, engineers can improve their robotic cars. However, there's no suggestion that robotic cars will be better than human-driven cars. And even if that seems reasonable to believe, it's too strong (and not supported by the stimulus) to say that they absolutely *would* be better.

2. (D) Paradox

Step 1: Identify the Question Type

The question asks for something that "helps to explain" something surprising, making this a Paradox question.

Step 2: Untangle the Stimulus

The stimulus presents information about a bird called the Common Loon. It breeds in certain breeding lakes, with each pair of birds usually getting its own lake. They get their own lake by finding one that's unoccupied or by kicking out a pair that got to the lake first. While it might seem easier to just find an empty lake, it turns out that, about half the time, they take the aggressive, kick-others-out approach. Adding to the mystery, they will take this option even when there are vacant lakes nearby.

Step 3: Make a Prediction

Take a moment to paraphrase this as a paradoxical question: If there are unoccupied lakes nearby, why go through all the trouble of confronting other birds and pushing them out? While it's not worth predicting an exact solution, know what the correct answer should do. It should show a benefit to taking the kick-the-other-birds out approach that makes it worth the effort.

Step 4: Evaluate the Answer Choices

(D) is correct. This suggests that, when they see another pair of birds, the loons take that as a sign that the lake is suitable for breeding. It might then be worth the effort rather than taking the risk of using one of the unoccupied lakes.

(A) is a 180. If most of the lakes in the area are suitable, then it makes it even more unusual that they would confront other birds rather than just going to one of the empty lakes.

(B) is Out of Scope. It doesn't matter if males or females are more prone to fighting. This does not address the question of why they would rather fight than find an unoccupied lake.

(C) is a 180. If they're frequently unsuccessful (they only win half the time), then why go through the trouble? There are plenty of unoccupied lakes that wouldn't require fighting.

(E) is irrelevant. It doesn't matter what makes the area suitable for breeding. The question remains: Why confront other birds rather than look for empty lakes, which might be equally suitable?

3. (B) Principle (Identify/Strengthen)

Step 1: Identify the Question Type

The question directly asks for a principle, and one that "most supports" the given reasoning. That makes this an Identify the Principle question, and one that works like a Strengthen question.

Step 2: Untangle the Stimulus

Despite customer complaints, the taxi driver concludes ([*s*]*o*) that it's a good idea to turn off the air conditioning while driving up a steep hill. The evidence is that keeping the air conditioning on would greatly decrease fuel economy.

Step 3: Make a Prediction

The taxi driver is choosing to sacrifice the comfort of air conditioning for the sake of retaining fuel economy. To support this decision, the taxi driver must be acting on a principle that fuel economy is more important than air conditioning (and thereby passenger satisfaction).

Step 4: Evaluate the Answer Choices

(B) is correct. This allows the air conditioning to be run when it doesn't impact fuel economy. However, when it does impact fuel economy, which happens when climbing steep hills, this gives the taxi driver the right to shut off the air conditioner—even if it upsets some passengers.

(A) is Out of Scope. The taxi driver's decision is based on preserving fuel economy, not maintaining a consistent speed.

(C) does not help. Even if the taxi wants to balance fuel economy concerns with customer concerns, this offers no justification for choosing fuel economy over customer concerns when it comes to running the air conditioner.

(D) is a 180. If the taxi driver always wants to satisfy customers, then the driver should keep the air conditioner on, not shut it off. That's what the customers want.

(E) is a 180. The passengers *did* complain, so this would not offer justification for turning the air conditioner off.

4. (A) Weaken

Step 1: Identify the Question Type

The question asks for something that "seriously weakens" the given argument, making this a Weaken question.

Step 2: Untangle the Stimulus

The author argues that Bach is remembered due to the sheer quantity of music he composed, not because he had such a high rate of top-quality music. The evidence is that, by the nature of him composing so much, he was bound to write *something* that was memorable.

Step 3: Make a Prediction

The author is arguing quantity over quality when it comes to explaining Bach's longevity. However, that assumes that the quantity Bach composed was enough to make him memorable, even if overall quality wasn't outstanding. To weaken this argument, the correct answer should show how the amount of work Bach composed, no matter how large it is, it's not enough to explain why Bach continues to be remembered.

Step 4: Evaluate the Answer Choices

(A) is correct. If other composers of Bach's time produced even *more* music, and they're not remembered, then quantity does not seem to be as likely an explanation as the author argues—in that case Bach's quantity did not mean it was *inevitable* that some would be outstanding.

(B) is not strong enough. Different people can be remembered for different reasons. So, even if there are some composers who produced few works but are still highly regarded, the author can still claim that Bach is different and is still remembered due to his prolific nature, not his overall quality.

(C) is irrelevant. Even if a lot of the mediocre works are forgotten, Bach's high-quality works are still remembered.

The question still remains: Why? Was it because those high-quality works made up a bigger proportion of Bach's work (contrary to the author's opinion)? Or was it because Bach composed so much music that he was bound to get lucky every now and then (as the author implies)? Without answering why, the validity of the author's argument cannot be judged.

(D) is irrelevant. It doesn't matter what the exact number is. If even the author's estimate of "more than a thousand" is enough to make Bach memorable, the author still has a point.

(E) is not strong enough. Even if some people are remembered because of their high ratio of great to not-so-great works, Bach could be different. Bach could be remembered because of his prolific nature, as the author suggests.

5. (E) Flaw

Step 1: Identify the Question Type

The question asks why the given argument is "vulnerable to criticism," which indicates a Flaw question.

Step 2: Untangle the Stimulus

The pundit concludes ([*c*]*learly*) that the city's two major political parties are now sharply divided on certain issues. The evidence is that the parties have been separated by less than 1 percent of the vote in each of the last four elections.

Step 3: Make a Prediction

The pundit makes quite a big scope shift. The evidence is merely about the voting records (i.e., how the public voted), while the conclusion is about the parties' stances on issues. These are two completely different ideas, and the pundit is unjustifiably suggesting that one impacts the other. The correct answer will expose this use of Mismatched Concepts.

Step 4: Evaluate the Answer Choices

(E) is correct, directly addressing the pundit's shift from voting results to the division on issues.

(A) is a Distortion. This suggests a causal error, and the pundit is implying causality (implying that a division of issues is causing the voting to be so evenly split). However, although the pundit does ignore alternative causes for why the vote is split, he does not confuse cause and effect. In this case, confusing a cause for an effect would mean the voting results actually caused the parties to become divided on the issues. However, that is not suggested.

(B) is Out of Scope. The pundit is not passing any judgment as to whether the situation is bad or acceptable.

(C) is not accurate. This describes Circular Reasoning. However, the evidence (about voting results) and the conclusion (about being divided on issues) are completely distinct.

(D) is Out of Scope. The argument only addresses the pundit's city. What is happening in other cities is irrelevant to the argument at hand.

6. (C) Strengthen

Step 1: Identify the Question Type
The question asks for something that "provides the most support" for the author's argument, making this a Strengthen question.

Step 2: Untangle the Stimulus
The author concludes ([*t*]*his suggests*) that the still waters around Shooter's Island are a nursery for young waterbirds. The evidence is that, despite having a similar overall waterbird population to other nearby islands, Shooter's Island has a lot more juveniles.

Step 3: Make a Prediction
The evidence merely cites population data, but is a high population of juveniles enough to claim that Shooter's Island serves as a nursery? The author assumes so, despite a lack of evidence about nurseries. To strengthen the argument, the correct answer must provide some evidence that the waters around Shooter's Island do, in fact, serve as a nursery.

Step 4: Evaluate the Answer Choices
(C) is correct. The waters around Shooter's Island are said to be exceptionally still. And if still waters are sought out as nurseries for juveniles, then that provides direct support for the author's conclusion.

(A) is irrelevant. It doesn't matter how long the shipwrecks have been in the area or how long the waters were still. There is still no evidence that the presence of many juveniles is indicative of a nursery.

(B) is irrelevant. Whether or not the population fluctuates at any of the islands in the area, this does nothing to confirm whether Shooter's Island is used as a nursery or not.

(D) is irrelevant. This makes the water around Shooter's Island unique in its stillness. However, there's still no evidence that this makes those waters a nursery.

(E) is a 180. The population around Shooter's Island is similar to the population around each of the other islands. If the population around nurseries is usually much greater, then Shooter's Island is likely *not* a nursery.

7. (C) Assumption (Necessary)

Step 1: Identify the Question Type
The question asks for an "assumption on which the … argument depends," making this a Necessary Assumption question.

Step 2: Untangle the Stimulus
The pollster concludes ([*s*]*o*) that making census participation voluntary would make opinion polls less accurate. The

evidence is that opinion polls should be based on a sample that adequately reflects the nation's demographics, and making census participation voluntary would decrease the number of people who participate.

Step 3: Make a Prediction
The pollster's argument is based on Mismatched Concepts. The conclusion is about the accuracy of poll results. By the first sentence, the pollster's claim of lower accuracy suggests that the sample group would be less reflective of the nation's demographics. However, the evidence mentions none of that, and merely addresses the number of people participating. The pollster must assume that these ideas are connected, namely that reducing the number of participants will make the sample group less reflective of the nation's demographics.

Step 4: Evaluate the Answer Choices
(C) is correct. By the Denial Test, if a voluntary census (which would have fewer participants) would *not* differ in its demographic makeup, then the results wouldn't change. The demographic makeup would be the same, thus contradicting the pollster's conclusion. The pollster must assume otherwise: The smaller sample size created by a voluntary census *would* be different.

(A) is a 180, at worst. If there were other ways to get a representational sample, then changing the number of people who take the national census could have no impact on opinion polls. Pollsters could start getting their sample groups from those other sources, instead.

(B) is not necessary. Perhaps the people who don't participate now avoid participating because they dislike the mandatory nature. Even if they change their mind and start participating if the census becomes voluntary, the overall participation could still drop, and the pollster would still have a point.

(D) is Out of Scope. It doesn't matter what the demographics are of the people who do *not* participate in polls or censuses. The pollster's argument only depends on the demographics of people who *do* participate.

(E) is irrelevant. It doesn't matter whether participation is consistent or wildly fluctuating with a mandatory census. As long as that participation level drops significantly with a switch to a voluntary census, then the pollster's argument still stands.

8. (E) Parallel Flaw

Step 1: Identify the Question Type
The question asks for reasoning that *parallels* the reasoning in the stimulus, and that reasoning is said to be *flawed*. That makes this a Parallel Flaw question

Step 2: Untangle the Stimulus

The author argues (*so*) that Hoitsu's "Spring and Autumn Maples" must be among the most valuable pieces in the museum's collection. The evidence is that light-sensitive pieces and the most valuable pieces will be displayed for only two weeks, and "Spring and Autumn Maples" will be displayed for only two weeks.

If	*sensitive OR most valuable*	→	*two weeks*

If	*two weeks*	→	*most valuable*

Step 3: Make a Prediction

The author makes two mistakes here. First, the author offers two characteristics of works that would suggest they'd be displayed for only two weeks (light-sensitive works or highly valuable ones), and then concludes that the work in question must be highly valuable. Why couldn't it be light-sensitive? The author overlooks that possibility. Furthermore, while being light-sensitive or highly valuable would warrant the two-week display time, those don't have to be the *only* characteristics that would limit the display time. There could be other, unmentioned reasons for displaying some works for only two weeks (e.g., the work is not very popular). The author ignores those other reasons as well. The correct answer will commit both of these errors. The author will offer two characteristics that would produce a particular result. The author will then arbitrarily choose one while also ignoring other options.

Step 4: Evaluate the Answer Choices

(E) is correct. The author offers two possible characteristics that would warrant a purple dot on a map (a historic monument or a hospital) and then arbitrarily decides a particular purple dot is a hospital and not a historic monument, while also ignoring that purple dots could be used for other types of buildings, as well.

(A) does not match. It is flawed—if the author's housing development is an existing structure, then it should be on the new map. However, this is not the same flaw as the original, which is based on offering two options for a situation and then ignoring one, as well as ignoring other unmentioned options.

(B) is not a match. Here, there are two different situations, and the same characteristic (a public building) produces a different result in each situation (blue dot on old maps, purple dot on new maps). With a different setup, the logic is not the same as the original.

(C) is not a match. In this situation, different characteristics (thoroughfares versus one-way streets) produce different results (solid lines versus dotted lines). This is not a parallel setup, and thus will not match the original argument.

(D) does not match. This does present two characteristics (city limits and thoroughfares) that produce the same result (a solid line). However, instead of erroneously choosing one over the other, the author here merely claims that you can't tell the difference. While potentially flawed (there may be other ways to distinguish the two other than line type), it's not the same flaw as the original.

9. (C) Flaw

Step 1: Identify the Question Type

The correct answer will describe why the argument given is "vulnerable to criticism," which is common language for a Flaw question.

Step 2: Untangle the Stimulus

The agent concludes ([*s*]*o*) that 90 percent of her clients had a ten-fold increase in profits. The evidence is that 90 percent of her clients who made a profit last year went from profits of $10,000 or less to profits of $100,000 or more.

Step 3: Make a Prediction

The math is good: $100,000 is ten times as much profit as $10,000. However, the agent illicitly shifted the scope of her argument. The evidence said this happened for 90 percent of her clients *who made a profit last year*. The conclusion is not about those clients. The conclusion is about *all* of her clients. So, what about the ones not mentioned? What about ones that took a loss last year, or worse, went bankrupt? By ignoring those companies, the agent is misrepresenting the success rate of her clients as a whole. She should have stuck with discussing only the profitable ones.

Step 4: Evaluate the Answer Choices

(C) is correct, exposing the scope shift from profitable companies to all companies.

(A) is irrelevant. It doesn't matter how much over $100,000 the profits were. Even if profits were $100,000.01, that's still "at least" 10 times as much as $10,000.

(B) is a Distortion. If only 90 percent of the clients saw a ten-fold increase, then there are another 10 percent that did not. However, it doesn't matter *why* they didn't see such a high increase. The argument is only about the numbers, not explanations for those numbers.

(D) is Out of Scope. This describes the commonly tested flaw of confusing necessity and sufficiency. However, the agent makes no mention of the conditions that created the profits, so there are no sufficient or necessary conditions to confuse.

(E) is Out of Scope. For the 10 percent of companies that failed to see a ten-fold increase in profits, it doesn't matter what their actual profits were. The agent might very well accept that some of their profits are still below $10,000. That doesn't impact the situation for the other 90 percent of the agent's profitable companies.

10. (D) Strengthen

Step 1: Identify the Question Type
The question asks for something that "helps to justify" a belief, making this a Strengthen question. It's useful to note that what's being strengthened is merely a belief and not necessarily an entire argument. So, there may not be any direct evidence, and the correct answer will have to provide that missing evidence.

Step 2: Untangle the Stimulus
The hospital officials' belief is at the very end: Discontinuing laundry services at the hospital will not put the patients at risk. As expected, there is no evidence for this belief. In fact, all that seems to exist is *counterevidence*. If the hospital staff has to wash clothes at home now, typical home washing machines do not get hot enough to kill off a certain dangerous bacterium.

Step 3: Make a Prediction
With only counterevidence to work with, this question works a lot like a Paradox question. If at-home washing machines don't get hot enough to kill off the dangerous bacterium, why do officials feel this plan is going to be risk-free for patients? Wouldn't the staff now come to work with bacterium-plagued uniforms? The author must assume there's another effective way to get rid of the bacteria and just omitted that evidence. To strengthen the officials' belief, the correct answer will provide the much-needed evidence.

Step 4: Evaluate the Answer Choices
(D) is correct. So, even if the washing machines don't kill the bacterium, staff are under strict orders to use dryers at a temperature that *is* hot enough to kill the bacterium. That would thus remove the risk and add support to the officials' claim.

(A) is irrelevant. Even if the staff are immune to the bacterium, the patients may not be. So, the staff would be safe if the bacterium was still on their clothes, but the patients would be at risk, contrary to the officials' belief.

(B) is a Distortion. Even if infected patients can be isolated, this still means that patients can be infected by the bacterium directly. That would mean the risk still exists, contrary to the officials' belief.

(C) is a 180, at worst. The evidence suggests that on-site washing machines *were* hot enough to kill off the bacterium. If most of the staff were using those machines and are now forced to use their at-home, not-hot-enough washing machines, then there is a big risk, contrary to the officials' claim.

(E) is Out of Scope. While this suggests that washing clothes at home could still kill off plenty of *other* harmful bacteria, the fact remains that the dangerous *Acinetobacter* is still going to survive. And that would still put patients at risk.

11. (A) Main Point

Step 1: Identify the Question Type
The question asks for the "conclusion drawn in the argument," making this a Main Point question.

Step 2: Untangle the Stimulus
The author mentions how many newspapers have started cutting back on book reviews, printing other features instead. The author then argues that this is not a wise decision. What follows is the evidence for why this is a bad move: It will alienate loyal readers in an attempt to attract people who don't want to read newspapers.

Step 3: Make a Prediction
As soon as the author passes judgment on the newspapers' plan, that's the main point. The first sentence merely describes the plan being judged, and the last sentence is evidence to support the author's judgment. The conclusion is: Cutting back on book reviews is ill-advised.

Step 4: Evaluate the Answer Choices
(A) is correct, accurately expressing the author's judgment against newspapers that are cutting back on book reviews.

(B) is just a fact. There's no evidence for this claim. It's just happening. This is not the author's point, which is to judge newspapers for performing this action.

(C) is evidence for why newspapers are cutting back on book reviews. It's not the author's conclusion.

(D) is the evidence in the last sentence that supports the author's conclusion, not the conclusion itself.

(E) is also part of the evidence in the last sentence. However, that merely supports the author's conclusion. It's not, itself, the conclusion.

12. (E) Assumption (Sufficient)

Step 1: Identify the Question Type
The question asks for something that, "if … assumed," will complete the argument. That makes this a Sufficient Assumption question.

Step 2: Untangle the Stimulus
The doctor starts off with the conclusion: More people in the area will get the flu this year than did last year. The evidence is that last year's flu strains are still present in the area, and some people in the area have already been infected by a new strain.

Step 3: Make a Prediction

The evidence is solely about the number of flu strains in the area. The conclusion, on the other hand, is about the number of *people* who will get infected. The evidence provides no details about that. All that's known is that some people (however many that is) are infected by the new strain. But how many people are going to be infected by the old strains? The doctor assumes that enough people will get infected by the old strains that, when combined with the people being infected by the new strain, will result in more people overall being infected by the flu.

Step 4: Evaluate the Answer Choices

(E) is correct. By this statement, the strains from last year will infect at least the same number of people this year. Add to that the people getting infected by the new strain this year, and you will definitely get a total greater than last year's total.

(A) is a 180, at worst. This suggests we can reduce the number of people who get infected by last year's strain. And if that reduction is large enough, it can more than compensate for however many people happen to get infected by this year's new strain.

(B) is Out of Scope. It doesn't matter how rare a new strain is. It's already appeared, and this does nothing to confirm whether the total number of people infected will be greater or less than last year.

(C) is Out of Scope. It doesn't matter whether the new strain is susceptible to the same approach or a different approach than last year's strains. **(C)** does not guarantee the conclusion because even if the new strain cannot be approached in the same way as last year's strains, perhaps a new way will be developed that helps keep infections down overall.

(D) is Out of Scope. The argument is not about how dangerous the flu is or the effect it has on people. The argument is solely about numbers: How many people will get infected?

13. (B) Point at Issue

Step 1: Identify the Question Type

The question asks for something about which two speakers "are committed to disagreeing," making this a Point at Issue question.

Step 2: Untangle the Stimulus

Hendry claims that most employee strikes should be legal. However, Hendry argues that university faculty should *not* be allowed to strike because it harms students. Hendry bases this argument on the principle that, if a strike would harm customers, the strike should be illegal. Menkin then questions Hendry's reasoning by pointing out how the principle would actually make almost all employee strikes illegal.

Step 3: Make a Prediction

The key here is not to assign a strong opinion to Menkin. Menkin says strikes should almost never be legal *if* Hendry's principle is correct. However, Menkin never actually argues whether or not the principle is actually correct. It's all hypothetical. What Menkin is really disagreeing about is how Hendry *applies* that principle. The principle states: If customers are harmed, the strike should not be legal. So, when Henry claims that most strikes *should* be legal, that implies (by contrapositive) that customers are usually not harmed by the strike. In contrast, Menkin suggests that the same principle would result in the opposite judgment: Most strikes should *not* be legal. By the principle, that implies that Menkin believes customers *are* usually harmed. And that's the point at issue.

Step 4: Evaluate the Answer Choices

(B) is correct. Menkin would agree that customers are being harmed, which is why Menkin argues that the principle suggests most strikes should *not* be legal. Hendry would disagree, as Hendry's first sentence indicates he finds most strikes should be legal, suggesting (by the principle) that customers are not being harmed.

(A) is Out of Scope for Menkin. Menkin does not mention any specifics on university students. If anything though, it's possible Menkin would likely agree that students should be considered customers because he says, based on the principle, almost no strikes should be permitted (which would likely include university strikes) because customers would be harmed (in this case, students). That would make this a potential point of agreement.

(C) is Out of Scope for Menkin. Menkin is only questioning the application of Hendry's principle. Menkin does not have any personal stake in whether or not university faculty should or should not strike.

(D) is a Distortion. Hendry directly makes this claim in the first sentence. And while Menkin seems to say the exact opposite in the last sentence, Menkin's argument is based on *if* Hendry's principle is correct. However, Menkin never says whether the principle is correct or not. If the principle is wrong, then Menkin may very well agree with Hendry, just not for the same reasoning.

(E), like **(A)**, is Out of Scope for Menkin. He does not directly address university issues at all. It's also conceivable this is a point of agreement. Hendry claims **(E)** is true: Students are harmed. And Menkin claims that the principle implies almost all strikes should be illegal. That would suggest Menkin feels that almost all strikes (likely including university strikes) do harm customers.

14. (E) Principle (Identify/Strengthen)

Step 1: Identify the Question Type
The question directly asks for a principle, and one that "helps to justify" the given reasoning. That makes this an Identify the Principle question, and one that works like a Strengthen question.

Step 2: Untangle the Stimulus
The author concludes ([c]*onsequently*) that uninformed viewers should not regard dramatic historical films as historically accurate. This is because such films rely on dramatic presentations and thus cannot provide evidence to support the film's accuracy.

Step 3: Make a Prediction
The author's claim about whether a film can be deemed historically accurate is based solely on whether or not that film can provide evidence for that accuracy. The author is acting on the principle that, if there's no evidence of a film's accuracy, then that film cannot be regarded as accurate. By contrapositive, if a film *is* regarded as accurate, then there must be evidence of that accuracy.

Step 4: Evaluate the Answer Choices
(E) matches the prediction, and is correct.

(A) is Out of Scope. Whether screenwriters add their own insight or not has no logical connection to the potential accuracy of the film, which is the point of this argument. Furthermore, the author's only recommendation is about what *viewers* should do, not what the *writers* should do.

(B) is a Distortion. The author would probably encourage adding more evidence to make something an accurate portrayal. However, **(B)** focuses on *documentaries*, whereas the stimulus focuses on historical dramas. Again, the author's only recommendation is for what *viewers* should do—not what the filmmakers should do. **(B)** does not justify claiming that the current *lack* of evidence in historical dramas means that they should *not* be deemed accurate.

(C) is Out of Scope. The author is not concerned about these films' suitability for educational purposes.

(D) is Out of Scope. The author is not concerned about whether or not such films should be entertaining.

15. (B) Point at Issue

Step 1: Identify the Question Type
The question presents two speakers and asks what they would "disagree over," making this a Point at Issue question.

Step 2: Untangle the Stimulus
Carrillo discusses a statistical model based on various pieces of information about primates. Carrillo argues that the conclusion about primates developing over 80 million years ago is strongly supported by the model. Olson is not so convinced. According to Olson, the oldest known primate fossils are only 55 million years old. An estimate of 81.5 million years is still nothing more than mere speculation.

Step 3: Make a Prediction
It's important to note that Olson is not saying that Carrillo is wrong, or that primates did not develop 81.5 million years ago. The real issue Olson has is Carrillo's overly enthusiastic claim that the statistical model "strongly supports" the 81.5 million figure. Olson does not see that figure as strongly supported. Olson calls it "sheer speculation." So, the real point at issue hinges on how convincing that model's estimate is.

Step 4: Evaluate the Answer Choices
(B) is correct. Carrillo argues that the model is very reliable, claiming it "strongly supports" the estimated origin of primates. Olson, on the other hand, calls it "sheer speculation," suggesting that the statistical method may not be as reliable as Carrillo implies.

(A) is a Distortion. Using the model, Carrillo definitely agrees with this statement. However, Olson's evidence is based on the oldest *known* primate fossils. Olson does not go so far as to say that primates have *not* been around longer. Olson may agree that primates have been around for some time longer than 55 million years. Olson just isn't convinced that it's as long as 81.5 million years, as Carrillo's model estimates.

(C) is Out of Scope. Carrillo mentions genetic diversity, but makes no connection between that and available fossils. Olson also mentions fossils, but makes no claims about their representation of diversity.

(D) is Out of Scope. Carrillo does not address or question the dating of Olson's fossils. Carrillo just claims that the statistical model predicts primates existing long before the date of Olson's fossils.

(E) is Out of Scope for Carrillo, who does not have any opinion about currently available fossils. Besides, Olson's fossils are merely said to be the oldest primate fossils that have currently been discovered. Neither author is suggesting they are fossils of the first primates to ever develop.

16. (B) Flaw

Step 1: Identify the Question Type
The question asks why the given argument is "vulnerable to criticism," making this a Flaw question.

Step 2: Untangle the Stimulus
The automobile executive argues that, contrary to what the critics claim, the cars' installed communications devices are not a dangerous distraction for drivers. The evidence is that drivers will use communications devices no matter what, and the installed devices are at least easier and (*hence*) safer to use.

Step 3: Make a Prediction

Sure, the installed devices might be *safer*, but that doesn't mean they're safe. That would be like saying getting hit on the head with a baseball doesn't hurt because it's less painful than getting hit by a brick. Either way, you're going to get hurt. Similarly, it doesn't matter if installed communication devices are safer than personal ones. Either way, such devices can still be dangerous. The executive fails to consider this, and thus provides an inadequate rebuttal to the critics' claim.

Step 4: Evaluate the Answer Choices

(B) is correct. Even if the installed devices are relatively safer, that doesn't change the fact that they could still be dangerous—and that's the substantive point that the executive fails to address properly.

(A) is Out of Scope. No principles are presented, and thus there are no principles to apply.

(C) is Out of Scope. This describes the flaw of confusing necessary and sufficient conditions. However, there are no conditional statements, and thus there is nothing that is deemed necessary for anything else.

(D) is a 180. The executive directly claims that the installed devices are safer than other devices.

(E) is Out of Scope. This describes the flaw of Circular Reasoning. However, the evidence about relative safety is adequately different from the conclusion regarding how distracting the devices are.

17. (C) Paradox

Step 1: Identify the Question Type

The question asks for something that will "resolve the apparent discrepancy" provided, making this a Paradox question.

Step 2: Untangle the Stimulus

According to the author, mosquito larvae are aquatic, so wet weather tends to bring about an increase in mosquito-borne diseases. There's an exception though (*however*). In wetland habitats, such diseases increase when there's a drought.

Step 3: Make a Prediction

There are a lot of hints here, so consider all of the information provided. The central mystery is this: If wet weather usually produces an increase in mosquito-borne diseases, why do mosquito-borne diseases increase in completely opposite conditions (a drought) in wetland areas? The increase in moist areas makes sense. Wet weather would produce a wet environment, giving mosquito larvae conditions to thrive. With more mosquitoes comes more diseases. Wetlands, on the other hand, are (as the name implies) usually wet. That should be a place for larvae to thrive all the time. So why would dry conditions lead to *more* mosquitoes in that area? It may be difficult to predict an exact answer. Instead, expect

the correct answer to show that something must change during droughts in the wetlands that benefits mosquitoes and allows them to flourish more than usual.

Step 4: Evaluate the Answer Choices

(C) is correct. In wetlands, wet conditions would make the area home to insects that eat mosquito larvae. That would keep mosquito populations down, and thus reduce the risk of disease. When the drought cuts down on predators, the mosquitoes might have a better chance to survive and spread disease.

(A) is a Distortion. This might explain why there are more mosquito-borne diseases in wetland areas, but it doesn't help explain why such diseases increase during droughts, which would not be ideal conditions for mosquito larvae.

(B) is a Distortion. The mystery is not about how many people are affected or get mosquito-borne diseases. The mystery is about why wetland mosquitoes spread diseases more during droughts than during other periods.

(D) is a Distortion. This may explain why there are more mosquito-borne diseases in wetland areas, but that's not the discrepancy. The discrepancy is about wetland mosquitoes spreading diseases more during droughts than during wet conditions.

(E) is Out of Scope. There's no logical connection between greater plant growth and mosquitoes. If mosquitoes are not affected by plants, then the increase in plant growth during droughts is irrelevant.

18. (D) Assumption (Necessary)

Step 1: Identify the Question Type

The question asks for an "assumption on which the argument relies," making this a Necessary Assumption question.

Step 2: Untangle the Stimulus

The author concludes ([*t*]*hus*) that emphasizing the dangers of a sedentary lifestyle would be more effective in getting people to exercise than would emphasizing the positive benefits of exercise. The evidence is that emphasizing the positive hasn't worked well so far, but emphasizing the negative has worked great for getting people to smoke less.

Step 3: Make a Prediction

The problem with the argument is that only one method (positivity) was tried with exercise, and only the other method (negativity) was tried with smoking. The author assumes that the key difference was the different techniques (it was the negativity that made the anti-smoking efforts more effective). However, it's equally possible that the key difference was the habit being addressed (exercise versus smoking). Perhaps changing people's smoking habits is just overall easier than changing people's exercise habits. The author overlooks that and assumes that negativity is the real key to success.

Step 4: Evaluate the Answer Choices

(D) is correct, suggesting that positive campaigns would not do better than negative campaigns; it's the negativity that made anti-smoking efforts more successful. By the Denial Test, if anti-smoking efforts *would* have been more successful with a positive campaign, then positive efforts would be more persuasive, and exercise campaigns would not get any better by switching to negativity. That would contradict the author, which means the author must assume otherwise: Positive efforts are *not* better.

(A) is an Irrelevant Comparison. It doesn't matter what the relative health risks are. The argument is about whether negative or positive efforts are more effective at influencing people to change their habits, regardless of the actual benefits or risks.

(B) is a Distortion. The effectiveness of delivering the message is of no importance. Even if the message was delivered loud and clear, it's still possible that people just didn't care enough to change their habits. The efforts have been to get people exercising more, not merely to inform them that exercise is good for them.

(C) is Out of Scope. This would not be surprising, as smoking campaigns have focused more on the negatives. However, even if everybody was aware of the benefits of quitting smoking, that does nothing to impact the author's conclusion about how negative campaigning could affect people's exercise habits.

(E) is a 180, at worst. If people are concerned about their health, then the current positive campaign for exercise, which focuses on health benefits, should do just fine. There would be no need or justification for switching to a negative campaign. Furthermore, **(E)** is not necessary to the author's argument. Put to the Denial Test, even if health concerns were a secondary concern for those that quit smoking, the campaign about health effects may still have effectively served to decrease smoking (at least in part), and thus the author's argument still holds up.

19. (A) Weaken

Step 1: Identify the Question Type

The question asks for the "strongest counter" Henry could make, making this a Weaken question.

Step 2: Untangle the Stimulus

Henry argues ([*t*]*herefore*) that, to reduce urban pollution, standard automobiles should be replaced with battery-powered cars. The evidence is that battery-powered engines produce less pollution than standard combustion engines. Umit argues otherwise. Batteries need to be recharged often, which will require more power from pollution-producing power plants.

Step 3: Make a Prediction

Umit's suggestion is that battery-powered cars would not change the overall urban pollution levels. Any pollution saved by changing engines would be immediately counteracted by additional pollution produced by power plants. However, Umit fails to show exactly how the different levels compare. If the additional pollution from power plants is not enough to compensate for the pollution saved by battery-powered engines, then Umit's argument fails. So, Henry could counter Umit effectively by showing how power plants will not produce enough counteracting urban pollution.

This should be enough to get started. However, there is a subtle shift in scope that would make the correct answer stand out even more—albeit a shift that may have been difficult to spot. Henry's conclusion is about the effect on *urban* pollution, not pollution as a whole. While Umit addresses the possibility of more pollution from power plants, that extra pollution would be irrelevant if it didn't contribute to urban pollution. So, Henry could also counter Umit's argument by showing how the extra pollution would not greatly impact pollution in urban areas.

Step 4: Evaluate the Answer Choices

(A) is correct, hinging on the subtle scope shift from urban pollution to overall pollution. If the power plants are located far away from cities, then the extra pollution produced is not as likely to impact urban pollution, and Umit's counterargument would be invalidated.

(B) is a 180. This is actually a subtle variation on the very point that Umit is arguing: The increased pollution from power plants and the decreased pollution from battery-powered engines would just cancel each other out. If this were true, then Umit's argument would still hold and Henry would be wrong: Overall pollution would not go down. To truly counter Umit's argument, Henry would have to show how the pollution decrease due to battery-powered engines would be *greater* than the increase from power plants. Just saying the two values are equal is not enough.

(C) is irrelevant. Even if Henry's plan was limited to smaller cars that require less power, the batteries would still need to be recharged. So it's still possible that the power needed to recharge those batteries is enough to produce more pollution than is saved by the battery itself.

(D) is irrelevant. Even if other options such as hybrid cars limit how much extra power is produced by power plants, the introduction of some battery-powered cars could still increase the demand for power just enough to compensate for any pollution saved by those batteries.

(E) is Out of Scope. Current demand doesn't matter. Even if the power plants can accommodate an increased demand, they will still produce more pollution, which is exactly the point that Umit is trying to make.

20. (B) Point at Issue

Step 1: Identify the Question Type

The question provides two speakers and asks for something they "disagree over," making this a Point at Issue question.

Step 2: Untangle the Stimulus

The student argues that it's unfair to prohibit students from citing online encyclopedias. The evidence is that students should be allowed to read whatever they want, and denying them that right would be censorship. The professor agrees that students can *read* whatever they want. The professor just suggests that online encyclopedias can't be *cited* because the lack of peer review makes those sources unreliable.

Step 3: Make a Prediction

The professor calls the student out for making an improper presumption. By making dramatic claims about censorship, the student is implying that the citation policy prevents students from reading what they want. However, the professor is quick to point out that the policy does not make any such implication. Of course students can read what they want. They just can't cite it. That's an entirely different statement. So, while there's a clear point of contention on the surface (the student finds the policy unfair, while the professor coolly suggests otherwise), their disagreement goes deeper. The disagreement is about whether the policy implies restrictions on what students can and cannot read.

Step 4: Evaluate the Answer Choices

(B) matches the prediction, and is correct.

(A) is a Distortion. The professor would agree with this, suggesting that cited references should be peer reviewed. However, the student does not dispute the claim that *some* references should be peer reviewed. The student just doesn't feel references should be *exclusively* peer reviewed.

(C) is Out of Scope. The student is only objecting to censoring references that are *not* peer reviewed. There is no discussion about whether censorship is justified for references that *are* peer reviewed.

(D) is Out of Scope. The student does not argue whether online encyclopedias have solid support or not. The only question is whether or not students can use them.

(E) is a 180. Both speakers agree that students *should* be allowed to read what they want. The issue is that the student feels the policy denies this right, while the professor argues that the policy does not deny that right.

21. (D) Strengthen/Weaken (Evaluate the Argument)

Step 1: Identify the Question Type

The question asks for something that would "help in evaluating" the given argument. This is an Evaluate the Argument question, which is a variation of Strengthen/Weaken questions. The correct answer will be a question that

addresses the finance minister's assumption such that the answer to that question will impact the validity of the argument.

Step 2: Untangle the Stimulus

The finance minister concludes ([*s*]*o*) that the country's "Doing Business" ranking will likely improve. The evidence is that "Doing Business" rankings are based on determining how difficult it would be for a hypothetical business to comply with regulations and tax laws, and the minister's country has recently made changes to make tax filing easier for small and midsized businesses.

Step 3: Make a Prediction

Unfortunately, the minister only mentions improvements for small and midsized businesses. The "Doing Business" ranking is based on a situation involving "a hypothetical business." If that hypothetical business is not small or midsized, then the changes made in the minister's country would be irrelevant. The correct answer should question the size of the hypothetical business to determine whether the country's changes are indeed relevant.

Step 4: Evaluate the Answer Choices

(D) is correct. If the hypothetical business is larger than what is considered midsized, then all of the changes in the minister's country are for naught. The ranking will likely go unchanged. However, if the hypothetical business is midsized or smaller, then the changes *would* be important, and the minister is justified in expecting a higher ranking.

(A) is Out of Scope. The rankings are said to be based solely on how difficult it is to pay taxes and comply with regulations. It doesn't matter how likely it is for new businesses to form.

(B) is Out of Scope. The rankings are based solely on the difficulty level of complying. It doesn't matter whether businesses actually comply or not.

(C) is an Irrelevant Comparison. The rankings are based on both tax filing and regulation compliance. It doesn't matter which is more difficult to do. If either one becomes easier (for the hypothetical business), then the ranking should improve.

(E) is Out of Scope. Who the minister is or was at any given time has no bearing at all on the difficulty of complying with the business laws.

22. (E) Flaw

Step 1: Identify the Question Type

The question asks why a line of reasoning is "vulnerable to criticism," which is common wording for a Flaw question.

Step 2: Untangle the Stimulus

The commentator is bothered by Roehmer, a very opinionated columnist who is having a polarizing effect on politics. The commentator complains that Roehmer attacks her opponent's motives and thus alienates those opponents. The commentator ends this diatribe by suggesting that Roehmer probably isn't bothered by any of this. After all, Roehmer only cares about pleasing her loyal readers.

Step 3: Make a Prediction
The commentator seems to have a lot of problems with Roehmer. However, at the end, the commentator seems particularly upset that Roehmer is unfazed by everything. And what is the basis for this observation? An attack on Roehmer's motives, claiming she only wants to please her readers. That's rather hypocritical seeing how, just two sentences earlier, the commentator complained about Roehmer attacking her opponents' motives. The correct answer should expose this hypocrisy.

It should be noted that this may have been a difficult flaw to predict, as it is not very frequently tested on the LSAT. Barring a solid prediction, have a basic understanding of the argument's structure and be ready to use elimination skills to home in on the correct answer.

Step 4: Evaluate the Answer Choices
(E) is correct. The commentator attacks Roehmer's motives, a tactic the commentator objected to earlier in the argument.

(A) is a Distortion. The cause and effect relationship here is not confused. Roehmer expresses her strong opinions, and divisiveness and alienation follow. There is no reason to suggest the causality goes the other way around.

(B) is Out of Scope. This suggests an *ad hominem* attack. However, the commentator is attacking Roehmer's actions, not her personal characteristics.

(C) is a Distortion. It is implied that Roehmer's actions are the cause of divisiveness and alienation, but it's not due merely to the time frame (one thing happened before the other). The evidence is based on so much more, including the partisan nature of Roehmer's opinions and Roehmer's willingness to attack her opponents' motives.

(D) is a Distortion. There is no contradiction. The column is consistently called out for being partisan and argumentative.

23. (E) Parallel Reasoning

Step 1: Identify the Question Type
The correct answer will be an argument "most similar" to the one in the stimulus, making this a Parallel Reasoning question.

Step 2: Untangle the Stimulus
The author argues that good short story writers are unlikely to be great novelists. The evidence is that short story writers have to masterfully deal with small details, while novelists have to focus on bigger issues, and very few writers can do both.

Step 3: Make a Prediction
The author is concluding that it's unlikely for a writer to excel at both short stories and novels because they each require different skills, and few people can master both skills. The correct answer will provide a similar structure of claiming that two fields require different skills, and arguing that it's unlikely for one person to possess both skills.

Step 4: Evaluate the Answer Choices
(E) is correct. While very vague, this exactly matches the structure of claiming that two fields can require different skills (one sport can require different skills than another), and arguing that it's *unlikely* for one person to possess both sets of skills.

(A) is Extreme. This suggests that a combination of two things will *never* happen. And this is based on evidence of what is *generally* or *usually* true, which makes the extreme conclusion unwarranted—a problem that was not present in the original argument.

(B) is not a match. This denies historians from accomplishing something based on some form of egotistical pride. ("I'm too gifted to spend time looking at what other people have done.") There are no skill sets that the author claims are rarely shared by one person.

(C) does not match. This argument makes a shift in scope. It says that painters cannot be objective scholars. It uses this to justify a conclusion that painters cannot be good scholars. However, there's no reason to believe that good scholars have to be objective. The original argument did not rely on any such assumption. Furthermore, **(C)** could be quickly eliminated because its conclusion is a definite *cannot*—whereas the conclusion from the stimulus had the more qualified *unlikely*.

(D) does not match. This just suggests that people, in general, are unlikely to succeed in a particular field. However, unlike the original argument, there is no second field with a different set of skills that the author claims is difficult to overlap.

24. (D) Flaw

Step 1: Identify the Question Type
The question asks why the "argument is flawed," making this a Flaw question.

Step 2: Untangle the Stimulus
The politician concludes ([*t*]*herefore*) that any of the regulations proposed by the Committee for Overseas Trade will help the country's economy. The evidence is that each proposed regulation will reduce the country's trade deficit, which is so large that it's weakening the economy.

Step 3: Make a Prediction
With the trade deficit having such a negative impact on the economy, it's reasonable to take action to reduce that deficit.

However, the politician may be overly optimistic in suggesting that reducing the deficit problem is suddenly going to turn the economy around. The politician overlooks the possibility that the reduction may not be enough to get the economy heading in the right direction. The politician also overlooks the possibility that other problems could exist or arise that would continue to hurt the country's economy. The correct answer will cite any overlooked possibility that suggests the economy might not bounce back as the politician expects.

Step 4: Evaluate the Answer Choices

(D) is correct, claiming that the effect of the regulations (reducing the deficit) can be counteracted by other effects. Thus, the economy may not improve, as the politician suggests.

(A) is a Distortion. The politician claims that the regulations will reduce the deficit, but that doesn't mean the deficit will increase without those regulations. It may just stay the same.

(B) is Extreme. The politician is only assuming that reducing the trade deficit will strengthen the economy. The politician does not claim this to be the *only* possible solution.

(C) is a Distortion. The politician is not appealing to authority. That would mean the politician accepts the proposals solely because the committee said to. However, the politician believes the regulations would help the economy because of the specific evidence about the anticipated reduction in the trade deficit by each of the proposals.

(E) is a Distortion. The argument is solely based on each regulation individually. There is no mention of putting all of the regulations together as a whole.

25. (D) Principle (Identify/Strengthen)

Step 1: Identify the Question Type

The question asks for a principle that would "help to justify" the given argument, making this an Identify the Principle question that works like a Strengthen question.

Step 2: Untangle the Stimulus

The essayist concludes ([*t*]*hus*) that it's too early to understand e-books as a medium. The evidence is that e-books are in a phase in which they are merely providing content available in print, so e-books have not evolved yet into their ultimate form.

Step 3: Make a Prediction

The conclusion mentions understanding e-books, but the evidence makes no mention of understanding. The evidence is only about e-books being at an early stage, yet to reach their ultimate form. The essayist assumes these ideas are connected, that e-books cannot be understood until they've reached their final stage. The correct answer will validate the argument by matching this logic, only in broader terms as to apply to other mediums as well.

Step 4: Evaluate the Answer Choices

(D) is a perfect match. As the essayist argues, this verifies that understanding a medium (e.g., e-books) requires seeing the full evolution of that medium. If that medium hasn't fully evolved (as e-books have yet to do), then it cannot be understood (as the essayist concludes about e-books).

(A) is a Distortion. This makes understanding a medium dependent on understanding the medium that came before it. In the case of e-books, that previous medium would be print books. However, there's no indication that we don't understand print books, so this can't justify the essayist's conclusion about e-books.

(B) is an Irrelevant Comparison. There's no reason to compare e-books to other electronic devices, and the argument is not based on one medium resembling another.

(C) is Out of Scope. It doesn't matter what's required to bring e-books to their ultimate form. This offers no justification for why the essayist believes e-books cannot be understood.

(E) is Out of Scope. It doesn't matter what is needed for one medium to replace another. This does nothing to justify the conclusion about whether a new medium (namely e-books) can be understood.

Section IV: Logic Games

Game 1: Flower Shop Shipments

Q#	Question Type	Correct	Difficulty
1	Must Be False (CANNOT Be True)	A	★
2	"If" / Must Be True	A	★
3	"If" / Could Be True EXCEPT	C	★
4	How Many	B	★
5	"If" / Must Be False	E	★
6	"If" / How Many	B	★★

Game 2: Architect Project Assignments

Q#	Question Type	Correct	Difficulty
7	Acceptability	D	★
8	Could Be True	E	★
9	"If" / Must Be False	B	★
10	Complete and Accurate List	E	★★
11	Must Be False (CANNOT Be True)	A	★

Game 3: Municipal Election Nominations

Q#	Question Type	Correct	Difficulty
12	Acceptability	E	★
13	"If" / Must Be True	E	★
14	Could Be True	B	★
15	Completely Determine	C	★★★
16	"If" / Must Be False (CANNOT Be True)	C	★
17	Rule Substitution	E	★★★

Game 4: Corporations Offering Bonds

Q#	Question Type	Correct	Difficulty
18	Acceptability	D	★
19	"If" / Must Be True	B	★★★
20	Could Be True	E	★★★
21	"If" / Could Be True	A	★★★
22	Could Be True	A	★★★
23	"If" / Must Be True	C	★★★★

KAPLAN

Game 1: Flower Shop Shipments

Step 1: Overview

Situation: A flower shop scheduling shipments

Entities: Eight kinds of flowers (lilies, mums, orchids, roses, sunflowers, tulips, violets, zinnias)

Action: Loose Sequencing. Determine the order in which the flowers are shipped. The game can only be recognized as Loose Sequencing by peeking ahead at the rules, all of which provide only relative relationships between entities. A Strict Sequencing game, by contrast, would have at least one rule dictating a fixed sequence (e.g., "A is exactly one space before B.") or referencing a specific position (e.g., "A is third.").

Limitations: There are eight shipments, each of which contains exactly one kind of flower, and each shipment contains a different flower. So, this is standard one-to-one sequencing.

Step 2: Sketch

Because this is a Loose Sequencing game, there is no need to draw a series of slots. Instead, list the entities by initial for now. The Master Sketch will be a tree diagram showing the connection between all of the entities.

L M O R S T V Z

Step 3: Rules

Rule 1 sets up a relationship between two entities: sunflowers at some point before orchids.

S — O

Rule 2 is a little more complex. One entity (orchids) will be shipped before each of three others (roses, violets, and zinnias). However, the order of the roses, violets, and zinnias remains undetermined.

O ⋜ R
   V
   Z

Rule 3 is another relationship between two entities: zinnias at some point before lilies.

Z — L

Rule 4 provides two more relationships: tulips before lilies, and tulips before mums. Similar to the situation with Rule 2, it cannot be determined whether lilies precede mums or vice versa.

T ⋜ L
  M

Step 4: Deductions

As with all Loose Sequencing games, the most significant deductions come from combining the rules through Duplication. In this game, every rule contains at least one entity that is duplicated in another rule. So, they can all be combined to create one all-encompassing diagram. If you did this while initially going through the rules, that's fine too, as long as you're careful not to skip any rules. If you're making the deductions after writing out each rule individually, it doesn't matter which rules you start with, but for this game, there was no reason to handle the rules out of order. The first two rules each mention orchids, so they can be combined: Sunflowers will be shipped before orchids (Rule 1), which in turn will be shipped before roses, violets, and zinnias, in any order (Rule 2).

S — O ⋜ R
      V
      Z

Zinnias are mentioned again in Rule 3. That allows that portion of the string to be extended, with lilies connected afterwards.

S — O ⋜ R
      V
      Z — L

Finally, lilies appear again in Rule 4. Tulips must be shipped before lilies. However, tulips have no connection to any of the other flowers from the previous rules. So, tulips will be added on a separate string before lilies. In addition, the tulips will also be shipped before the mums, which are not connected to anything else. So, the mums will be added on a separate string after tulips.

S — O ⋜ R
      V
      Z — L
      T ⋜ M

Before answering the questions, consider two things: What could be shipped first, and what could be shipped last? To be shipped first, a flower cannot be preceded by any other flower. Only sunflowers and tulips have no connections before them, so only sunflowers or tulips can be shipped first. On the other hand, lilies, mums, roses, and violets all have no connections after them. So, any of those four flowers could be shipped last.

Step 5: Questions

1. (A) Must Be False (CANNOT Be True)

The correct answer will be a kind of flower that cannot be among the first four shipped. The remaining choices will list flowers that could be among the first four shipped.

To be prevented from shipping fourth, a flower would need too many flowers shipped before it (pushing it too late to be shipped fourth) or too many after it (requiring it to ship too early to be fourth). Lilies must be shipped after both zinnias (Rule 3) and tulips (Rule 4), and zinnias must ship after orchids (Rule 2), which in turn must ship after sunflowers (Rule 1). That's four flowers that must be shipped before lilies, and that's too many for lilies to ship fourth. Even if those four flowers were the first four shipped, lilies still couldn't be shipped until fifth, at earliest—never fourth. That makes **(A)** correct.

For the record, mums need only be shipped after tulips (Rule 4). So, if tulips were shipped first, mums could be shipped second—definitely among the first four. That eliminates **(B)**. And roses, violets, and zinnias are each only restricted by sunflowers and orchids beforehand. So, if sunflowers and orchids were shipped first and second, respectively, any of roses, violets, or zinnias could be shipped third (i.e., among the first four). That eliminates **(C)**, **(D)**, and **(E)**.

2. (A) "If" / Must Be True

For this question, tulips are established as the sixth shipment. That creates a strict assignment. So, draw out eight slots, and add T to the sixth. That leaves two slots after T, which must be filled by lilies and mums, in either order (Rule 4).

$$\underline{\quad}\ \underline{\quad}\ \underline{\quad}\ \underline{\quad}\ \underline{\quad}\ \underline{T}\ \underline{L/M}\ \underline{M/L}$$
$$\ 1\quad 2\quad 3\quad 4\quad 5\quad 6\quad 7\quad\ \ 8$$

Everything else must be among the first five shipments, namely, sunflowers, orchids, roses, violets, and zinnias. Sunflowers must be shipped before the rest, so sunflowers will be shipped first. After that, orchids have to be shipped before the rest, so orchids will be shipped second. That leaves roses, violets, and zinnias, which can be shipped in any order.

$$\overset{\textstyle R,\ V,\ Z}{\underline{S}\ \underline{O}\ \overbrace{\underline{\quad}\ \underline{\quad}\ \underline{\quad}}\ \underline{T}\ \underline{L/M}\ \underline{M/L}}$$
$$\ 1\quad 2\quad 3\quad 4\quad 5\quad 6\quad 7\quad\ \ 8$$

Orchids are definitely shipped second, making **(A)** correct. The remaining choices are all possible, but need not be true.

3. (C) "If" / Could Be True EXCEPT

For this question, orchids are established as the fourth shipment. Draw out eight slots, and add orchids to the fourth. After orchids, roses, violets, and zinnias must be shipped, and lilies will be shipped after the zinnias. So, those four flowers must take up the sole four slots after orchids in the sketch. That leaves three slots before orchids, which must be occupied by the remaining flowers: sunflowers, tulips, and mums.

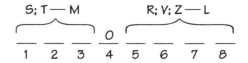

Among the first three flowers, tulips have to ship before mums. So, tulips cannot be shipped third and mums cannot be shipped first. Among the last four flowers, zinnias need to ship before lilies. So, zinnias cannot ship last and lilies cannot ship fifth. Otherwise, there would be no room to squeeze zinnias between the orchids and the lilies. Because of that, **(C)** is impossible and is thus the correct answer.

4. (B) How Many

The question asks for the number of kinds of flowers that could possibly be shipped second. One way to start is to eliminate the ones that certainly cannot be shipped second. That list includes roses, which need to be shipped after both orchids (Rule 2) and thereby sunflowers too (Rule 1). So, even if sunflowers and orchids were the first two shipments, roses couldn't be shipped any sooner. The same is true for violets and zinnias. And by Rule 3, lilies must ship even later, so they couldn't possibly be shipped second, either. With roses, violets, zinnias, and lilies out of the running, that leaves only four kinds of flowers to test: mums, orchids, sunflowers, and tulips. That alone eliminates **(C)**, **(D)**, and **(E)**.

Before drawing a ton of sketches, look at previous work to save a lot of time. In the second question of the set, it was determined that orchids could be shipped second, and in the third question, the second shipment could have been any of sunflowers, tulips, or mums. So, without further testing, any of the four remaining flowers could be shipped second, making **(B)** correct.

Without using previous work, it could be noted that neither sunflowers nor tulips have to be shipped after anything else, so either one could be shipped first. Whichever one is shipped first, the other could then be shipped second. And orchids and mums each only have to preceded by a single other flower (sunflowers and tulips, respectively). So, if sunflowers were shipped first, orchids could be second. And if tulips were shipped first, mums could be second.

5. (E) "If" / Must Be False

For this question, zinnias are established as the seventh flower to be shipped. Draw eight slots, and add Z to the seventh. By Rule 3, lilies must be shipped last.

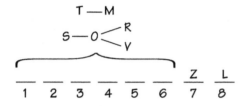

Unfortunately, that's as much as can be established for sure. Everything else will take up the first six slots, but there are two separate strings to keep track of. First, sunflowers must still ship before orchids, which in turn must ship before both roses and violets (in either order). Those four flowers will take up four of the first six shipments. The remaining shipments will be tulips and mums, in that order. They could take up any pair of slots. However, tulips could not be shipped sixth. That would leave no more shipments for the mums. That makes **(E)** impossible, and thus the correct answer.

6. (B) "If" / How Many

For this question, zinnias will be shipped third. Draw eight slots, and add Z to the third. Orchids must be shipped before zinnias (Rule 2), and sunflowers must be shipped before zinnias (Rule 1). Thus, sunflowers and orchids will be shipped first and second, respectively.

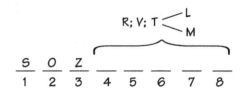

And that is as much as can be established. The question asks for the number of flowers that could be shipped fourth, i.e., the first open slot remaining. Consider what flowers remain. There are roses and violets, neither of which have any restrictions now that sunflowers and orchids are established. So, either of those kinds of flowers could be fourth.

And then there are tulips, lilies, and mums. Lilies and mums cannot be shipped until tulips are shipped, so neither of those could be shipped fourth at this point. However, tulips don't have to ship after anything, so they could also be shipped fourth. In summary, the fourth shipment could be roses, violets, or tulips—a total of three possibilities. That makes **(B)** correct.

Game 2: Architect Project Assignments

Step 1: Overview

Situation: Architects being assigned projects

Entities: Four architects (Fredericks, Guerrero, Horowitz, Lee) and four projects (W, X, Y, Z)

Action: Strict Sequencing (Double). Determine the order in which the projects are completed, and thus the order in which the architects complete the projects. In essence, there will be two distinct sequences occurring simultaneously. Some might classify this game as a Hybrid of Sequencing (order the projects) along with either Matching or Distribution (assign the architect). Those are reasonable labels, even if such games are slightly different in how they operate. However, whatever you call it, the resulting sketch would be identical (two sets of four dashes), so the specific classification is not essential here.

Limitations: Each architect gets one unique project, and each project is finished at a different time. So, the sequencing is one-to-one.

Step 2: Sketch

Set up two rows of four slots, one on top of the other. Write the architects' initials next to one row and the project initials next to the other. Make sure the slots line up vertically so that each project-architect pairing is clearly visible.

$$\begin{array}{c|cccc} & 1 & 2 & 3 & 4 \\ \hline F\,G\,H\,L & \_\_ & \_\_ & \_\_ & \_\_ \\ w\,x\,y\,z & \_\_ & \_\_ & \_\_ & \_\_ \end{array}$$

Step 3: Rules

Rule 1 creates a two-option block. One point in the sequence will be either Fredericks or Lee with project Z:

Rule 2 provides some Formal Logic. If Guerrero is not assigned to project W, then Fredericks is. By contrapositive, if Fredericks does not get project W, Guerrero does. Instead of writing this all out, consider the implication. If either Fredericks or Guerrero does not get assigned to W, the other one does. In short, this means that one of those two (Fredericks or Guerrero) must be assigned to W. That creates a block similar to the one created by Rule 1.

Rule 3 is more Formal Logic, but this one involves multiple projects. If Fredericks is not assigned to project W, Horowitz *is* assigned to project Y. By contrapositive, if Horowitz is not assigned to project Y, then Fredericks *is* assigned to project W.

Rule 4 finally gets down to the sequencing, creating a temporal block: Fredericks will finish immediately before Guerrero.

Rule 5 establishes Horowitz as the last architect to finish. Add H to the final slot in the architect row of the sketch.

Step 4: Deductions

The first thing to notice is that each of the first four rules mentions Fredericks. That suggests Fredericks is very important to this game. One valuable deduction to notice is that Fredericks is limited to two positions in the sequence. Because Horowitz finishes fourth (Rule 5), Fredericks cannot finish fourth, nor can Fredericks finish third (Rule 4). Fredericks could only finish first (which would make Guerrero second, leaving Lee as third) or second (which would make Guerrero third, leaving Lee as first). So, the sequence of architects can only be F, G, L, H or L, F, G, H.

However, the more valuable information may come from the possible pairings of the projects. Rules 2 and 3 indicate a connection between Fredericks (the most significant architect in the game) and project W. Whether or not Fredericks gets assigned to project W, the impact is noticeable. Consider both scenarios. If Fredericks does not get assigned to project W, then Guerrero does (Rule 2), and Horowitz gets project Y (Rule 3). That leaves project X or Z for Fredericks (who will finish immediately before Guerrero with project W), and the remaining project is left for Lee. Either way, Rule 1 is satisfied.

$$\text{I)} \quad \begin{array}{cccc} 1 & 2 & 3 & 4 \\ \_\_ & \_\_ & \_\_ & \boxed{\text{H}} \;\boxed{\begin{array}{c}F\\x/z\end{array}} \boxed{\begin{array}{c}G\\w\end{array}} \boxed{\begin{array}{c}L\\z/x\end{array}} \\ \_\_ & \_\_ & \_\_ & y \end{array}$$

If Fredericks does get assigned to project W, then Lee must get project Z (Rule 1). Guerrero will immediately follow

Fredericks with either project X or Y, and Horowitz will finish last with the remaining project.

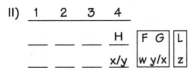

There are practically two sets of Limited Options here: one for the sequence of architects, and one for the assignment of architects to projects. These could be combined to form four options. However, that's a lot of options to draw, and perhaps too much effort for a game that only has five questions. Drawing out the Limited Options for either just the sequence of architects or just the architects' assignments (as we did here) could be helpful. However, even if you didn't draw out either variation of the Limited Options, taking the time to consider the implications of the rules and significance of Fredericks should be enough to efficiently tackle the questions.

Step 5: Questions

7. (D) Acceptability

As with any Acceptability question, go through the rules one at a time, and eliminate answers that violate the rules.

(A) violates Rule 1 by giving Z to Guerrero. **(E)** violates Rule 2 because Guerrero does not get W, but it's then given to Lee instead of Fredericks. **(C)** violates Rule 3 because Fredericks is not assigned W, but Horowitz is assigned X instead of Y. **(B)** violates Rule 4 by getting Fredericks and Guerrero in the wrong order. No need to test Rule 5. Only **(D)** remains, and is the only acceptable answer.

8. (E) Could Be True

The correct answer will be the only one that could be true. The remaining four choices will certainly be false.

Every choice here hinges entirely on the order of the architects and not the projects, so only Rules 4 and 5 are relevant. And a quick check shows that all of the wrong choices here violate Rule 4. **(A)** is impossible as Guerrero must be preceded by Fredericks and thus cannot finish first. And **(B)**, **(C)**, and **(D)** all violate the Fredericks-Guerrero block by placing Fredericks immediately before or Guerrero immediately after the wrong person. Only **(E)** is possible. This could also be quickly confirmed by reviewing the only two possible sequences determined while making deductions (F, G, L, H or L, F, G, H).

9. (B) "If" / Must Be False

For this question, X is completed last, which is when Horowitz finishes (Rule 5). This is only possible in Option II because Option I has Y assigned to Horowitz. If you didn't set up the Limited Options, walk through the subsequent deductions to determine the architects' assignments. Because Horowitz is assigned X and not Y, Fredericks must be assigned W (Rule 3). That means Lee must be assigned Z (Rule 1), leaving Y for Guerrero. All that's left is to determine the order. Horowitz is last. Fredericks and Guerrero, in that order, are consecutive. So, the order is either F, G, L, H or L, F, G, H. With the assignments determined, that creates two options:

IIa)

	1	2	3	4
	F	G	L	H
	w	y	z	x

IIb)

	1	2	3	4
	L	F	G	H
	z	w	y	x

Based on that, W cannot be completed third, making **(B)** the correct answer. The remaining answers all could be true.

10. (E) Complete and Accurate List

The correct answer to this question will be a list of every architect who could possibly be assigned to project X. Not all at once, of course, as only one person is assigned to each project. However, the correct answer must list every person who can, leaving nobody out.

By the rules, no restriction is placed on project X. And sure enough, looking over the possible assignments determined while making deductions, it appears any of the four architects could be assigned to X. In testing when Fredericks is assigned to W, Lee is assigned to Z, and either Guerrero or Horowitz could be assigned to X. And when Fredericks is not assigned to W, either Fredericks or Lee could be assigned to X. So the complete list should be all four architects, which is **(E)**.

11. (A) Must Be False (CANNOT Be True)

The correct answer will be the one that is impossible. The remaining answers could all be true.

By Rule 5, Horowitz finishes last. By Rule 2, project W will be assigned to either Guerrero or Fredericks—never Horowitz. So, W will never be completed last, making **(A)** the correct answer. The remaining answers are all possible.

Game 3: Municipal Election Nominations

Step 1: Overview

Situation: Selecting nominees for a municipal election

Entities: Three offices (mayor, treasurer, councillor) and six people (Frost, Grant, Hu, Jensen, Kuno, Llosa)

Action: Selection/Distribution Hybrid. Determine which people will be nominated to run for office (Selection) and assign them to the office for which they will run (Distribution).

Limitations: Exactly four of the six people will be selected. When distributed, one will run for mayor, one for treasurer, and two for councillor.

Step 2: Sketch

Start by listing the entities by initial. For the selection component, set up an In/Out table. The Out column should have two slots for the two people not selected. The In side should be split into three columns for the distribution, adding the appropriate number of slots for each position.

F G H J K L

may	treas	coun	out
—	—	—	—
		—	—

Step 3: Rules

Rule 1 provides some Formal Logic affecting only the selection. If Frost is nominated, then Grant is not. By contrapositive, if Grant is nominated, then Frost is not. In short, if one of them is nominated, the other is out. That means they can't both be nominated, i.e., at least one of them is out. Instead of writing this rule off to the side, add it to the sketch. Draw "F/G" into one of the out slots. Note that it's possible for both to be out, but only one is certain.

Rule 2 provides more Formal Logic, this time affecting the distribution. If Hu is a councillor nominee, then Jensen is a mayoral nominee. By contrapositive, if Jensen is not a mayoral nominee, then Hu is not a councillor nominee.

$$\frac{coun}{H} \longrightarrow \frac{may}{J}$$

$$\sim\frac{may}{J} \longrightarrow \sim\frac{coun}{H}$$

Rule 3 limits the treasurer nominee to Frost or Hu. Add "F/H" to the treasurer column.

Rule 4 dictates that Kuno cannot be a councillor nominee. Add "~K" beneath the councillor column.

Step 4: Deductions

The nature of these rules makes it difficult to find any major deductions. The first two rules are conditional, which usually

are not useful for making deductions. If something triggers the logic, then there are deductions to be made. However, if the logic is not triggered, there are no deductions.

Rule 3 suggests the potential for Limited Options. However, it makes almost no difference whether Frost or Hu is treasurer. Only if Frost is treasurer can any deduction be made (that, by Rule 1, Grant is out).

And, by kicking Kuno out of a councillor position, Rule 4 leaves only two options for Kuno: nominee for mayor, or not nominated at all. However, again, neither option provides enough concrete deductions to warrant drawing Limited Options.

There are no Blocks of Entities and no Established Entities. Numbers will be important but do not provide any deductions of substance here. And Frost and Hu are duplicated in the rules but not in any particularly useful way. Also worth noting is that that there are no rules about Llosa, so she is the game's lone Floater.

Step 5: Questions

12. (E) Acceptability

As with any Acceptability question, go through the rules one at a time, and eliminate answers as they violate those rules.

(A) violates Rule 1 by having Frost as a nominee, but also having Grant as a nominee. **(D)** violates Rule 2 by having Hu as a nominee for councillor but giving the mayoral nomination to Kuno instead of Jensen. **(C)** violates Rule 3 by giving the treasurer nomination to Grant instead of Frost or Hu. **(B)** violates Rule 4 by nominating Kuno for councillor. That leaves **(E)** as the only possible answer, and thus the correct one.

13. (E) "If" / Must Be True

For this question, Grant is nominated as a councillor. For starters, nominating Grant means Frost is not nominated at all (Rule 1). With Frost out, only Hu can be nominated for treasurer (Rule 2).

may	treas	coun	out
—	H	G	F
		—	—

That makes **(E)** correct.

14. (B) Could Be True

The correct answer will be two people who could, together, be the two nominees for councillor. Start by considering the rules. By Rule 1, Frost and Grant cannot both be nominated. That eliminates **(A)**. By Rule 2, if Hu is nominated for councillor, Jensen would have to be nominated for mayor, not councillor. That eliminates **(D)**. And Kuno cannot be a councillor nominee, by Rule 4. That eliminates **(E)**.

That leaves **(B)** and **(C)**. Test one. If it works, then that's the correct answer. If it doesn't, then the other answer must be correct. If Frost and Jensen were councillor nominees, then Hu would be nominated for treasurer (Rule 3). With Frost nominated, Grant would be out (Rule 1). However, the mayoral nominee could still be Kuno or Llosa. The remaining person would be out.

may	treas	coun	out
K/L	H	F	G
		J	L/K

Nothing is violated here, so this could be true. That makes **(B)** the correct answer. For the record, if Grant and Hu were nominated for councillor, that would leave Frost as the nominee for treasurer (Rule 3). However, this violates Rule 1 by having both Frost and Grant as nominees.

15. (C) Completely Determine

The correct answer will be the one that allows for the entire assignment of nominees to be determined with absolute certainty. In other words, it will be known exactly who is nominated and to which positions they are nominated. The twist here is that the person listed in the correct answer will be someone who is *not* nominated. So, if that person is out, everything else will be completely mapped out.

(A) and **(B)** list Frost and Grant. By Rule 1, it was always known that one of these two would be out. However, knowing which one is out has no real impact on the game. In fact, sketches for the second and third questions result in Frost and Grant not being nominated, with no complete sketches. For those reasons, **(A)** and **(B)** are eliminated.

(C) lists Hu. If Hu is out, that leaves Frost as the nominee for treasurer (Rule 3). With Frost in, Grant is out. So, the two people out are Grant and Hu. That means everyone else (Frost, Jensen, Kuno, and Llosa) are nominated. Frost is the treasurer nominee. Kuno cannot be a councillor nominee, so Kuno will be the mayoral nominee. That means Jensen and Llosa are the councillor nominees.

may	treas	coun	out
K	F	J	G
		L	H

With the sketch fully complete, that makes **(C)** correct. For the record:

If Jensen or Kuno were not nominated, it's not possible to determine whether Frost or Grant is the second person not nominated. That uncertainty eliminates **(D)** and **(E)**.

16. (C) "If" / Must Be False (CANNOT Be True)

For this question, Kuno is one of the nominees. By Rule 4, Kuno cannot be nominated for councillor. And by Rule 3, Kuno cannot be nominated for treasurer. Thus, Kuno is the nominee for mayor. Because of that, the contrapositive of Rule 2 is triggered. Jensen is not the nominee for mayor, so that means Hu cannot be a nominee for councillor.

may	treas	coun	out
K	—	—	—
		—	—

~H

That makes **(C)** the correct answer.

17. (E) Rule Substitution

The correct answer here will be a new rule that could be swapped with the last rule (Kuno cannot be a councillor nominee) without changing the game in any way. In other words, if the last rule were replaced with the correct answer, the same restriction would be established without adding any new restrictions.

By denying Kuno a councillor nomination, the original rule effectively limited Kuno to two options: mayoral nominee or not nominated at all. (After all, Rule 3 already denies Kuno a shot as the treasurer nominee.) Recognizing this from the beginning makes **(E)** stand out as a quick and effective replacement for the original rule. It's exactly how the original rule restricted Kuno, without adding any unnecessary restrictions. That makes **(E)** the correct answer. For the record:

(A) is both too restrictive and not restrictive enough. The original rules allowed other mayoral candidates, and limiting the mayoral candidate to Jensen or Kuno does not prevent Kuno from being a councillor nominee should Jensen get the mayoral nod. **(B)** would not restrict Kuno from being a councillor. Kuno could join one of Jensen or Llosa as the other nominee. With Rule 4 removed, and **(B)** added, this would be possible, which eliminates **(B)**.

may	treas	coun	out
J/L	H	L/J	F
		K	G

(C) and **(D)** kick out Kuno under certain conditions (Frost nominated or Hu as a councillor). However, if those conditions are not met, the rules leave no restriction on Kuno, so there's no guarantee Kuno will be denied a councillor nomination, as the original rule required. That eliminates **(C)** and **(D)**.

Game 4: Corporations Offering Bonds

Step 1: Overview

Situation: Corporations offering bonds

Entities: Six corporations whose names don't sound made up at all (Goh Industrials, HCN, Lorilou, RST, SamsonGonzales, VELSOR) and two bond types (5-year and 10-year)

Action: Matching. Determine which corporations offer 5-year bonds and which ones offer 10-year bonds.

Limitations: Each bond type is offered by exactly four corporations. Each corporation offers at least one bond. Two will offer both bond types, which means the remaining four will offer exactly one each.

Step 2: Sketch

For this game, it makes the most sense to set up two columns, one for each bond type. After all, it is given that each bond type will be offered by exactly four corporations, so each column can be populated with four slots. If the columns were set up by corporation, each column would get one slot, but it would be unknown which columns get the extra slots. So, list the corporations by initial and set up the two columns for the bonds.

$$
\begin{array}{c}
\text{G H L R S V} \\[4pt]
\begin{array}{c|c}
5 & 10 \\
\hline
\_\_ & \_\_ \\
\_\_ & \_\_ \\
\_\_ & \_\_ \\
\_\_ & \_\_ \\
\end{array}
\end{array}
$$

Step 3: Rules

Rule 1 prevents HCN and Lorilou from offering the same type of bond. This could be noted to the side. However, there's a more useful interpretation. There are only two types of bonds, and each corporation has to offer at least one. By this rule, whichever bond HCN offers, Lorilou will have to offer the other, and vice versa. So, these corporations can only offer one bond each. One will offer a 5-year bond, the other a 10-year bond. Add "H/L" to one slot in each column.

$$
\begin{array}{c|c}
5 & 10 \\
\hline
\text{H/L} & \text{L/H} \\
\_\_ & \_\_ \\
\_\_ & \_\_ \\
\_\_ & \_\_ \\
\end{array}
$$

In addition, because neither of these corporations can offer both bonds, you can mark up the entity list. Add a "1" above H and L, or even cross them out as they've already been established (to some degree) in the sketch and will not be reused.

Rule 2 provides some Formal Logic. If VELSOR offers 5-year bonds, then SamsonGonzales offers both. By contrapositive, if SamsonGonzales does not offer both bond types (i.e., offers only one), then VELSOR cannot offer 5-year bonds (i.e., must offer only 10-year bonds).

$$
\frac{5}{V} \longrightarrow \frac{5}{S} \; \& \; \frac{10}{S}
$$

$$
\sim\!\frac{5}{S} \; \text{OR} \; \sim\!\frac{10}{S} \longrightarrow \sim\!\frac{5}{V}\left(\frac{10}{V}\right)
$$

Note: It's important that the contrapositive not simply suggest that VELSOR offers the 10-year bonds. Because some corporations can offer both, it has to be clear that VELSOR will *not* also offer 5-year bonds if SamsonGonzales is limited to just one.

Rule 3 provides more Formal Logic. If Lorilou offers 10-year bonds, then RST does, too. By contrapositive, if RST does not offer 10-year bonds, then Lorilou cannot offer 10-year bonds.

$$
\frac{10}{L} \longrightarrow \frac{10}{R}
$$

$$
\sim\!\frac{10}{R} \longrightarrow \sim\!\frac{10}{L}
$$

Note: In the contrapositive, you cannot change it to read "If RST offers 5-year bonds, then so does Lorilou." This is because if RST does offer 5-year bonds, it could *still* offer 10-year bonds as well. In that case, Lorilou could offer 10-year bonds and that's it. There would be no need for Lorilou to offer 5-year bonds.

Step 4: Deductions

With only three rules, there is not a lot to work with. There are no Blocks of Entities. The first rule offers a potential for Limited Options; however, there's only a deduction if Lorilou offers 10-year bonds (Rule 3 would require RST to offer 10-year bonds, as well). That one minor deduction is not enough to warrant drawing out two whole sketches. The Established Entities of HCN and Lorilou offer no concrete deductions. Number restrictions have been accounted for: HCN and Lorilou each offer only one bond, but it still cannot be determined which corporations will offer both. And Lorilou is the only duplicated entity. However, as already mentioned, it does not offer any substantial deductions. Instead, use the New-"If" questions to draw sketches as needed and make sure to keep referencing the rules.

Step 5: Questions

18. (D) Acceptability
As usual with Acceptability questions, go through the rules one at a time. Eliminate answer choices that violate those rules until only one answer—the correct one—remains.

(C) violates Rule 1 by having HCN and Lorilou both offer 10-year bonds. **(E)** violates Rule 2 by having VELSOR offer 5-year bonds, but SamsonGonzales only offering one bond type. **(A)** violates Rule 3 by having Lorilou offer 10-year bonds, but not RST. And ... that's all of the rules.

That leaves two choices that do not violate any of the rules. In a case like this, one choice must violate a restriction from the overview. In this case, **(B)** has the same four companies offer both bond types. Only two companies are supposed to do that, and this leaves two companies out altogether (Lorilou and RST). That eliminates **(B)**, leaving **(D)** as the only acceptable answer.

19. (B) "If" / Must Be True
For this question, neither Lorilou nor VELSOR offer 5-year bonds. That means the other four companies, Goh Industrials, HCN, RST, and SamsonGonzales must be the four that offer 5-year bonds, leaving Lorilou and VELSOR to offer 10-year bonds. With Lorilou offering 10-year bonds, RST must also offer 10 year-bonds (Rule 3).

5	10
H	L
G	V
R	R
S	—

The last corporation offering 10-year bonds cannot be HCN (Rule 1), but it could be either Goh Industrials or SamsonGonzales. However, the questions asks for what *must* be true, and that's **(B)**—RST definitely offers both bonds.

20. (E) Could Be True
The question asks for two corporations that could be the two offering both types of bonds. Rule 1 makes it impossible for either HCN or Lorilou to offer both types. That eliminates **(A)** and **(C)**.

The remaining choices all include VELSOR. If VELSOR offered both bonds, that would include the 5-year bonds. In that case, by Rule 2, SamsonGonzales would have to be the other corporation offering both bonds. That means only **(E)** is possible, and thus the correct answer.

21. (A) "If" / Could Be True
For this question, SamsonGonzales and VELSOR must offer different types of bonds. That means each one can only offer one type of bond. In that case, by Rule 2, VELSOR cannot offer 5-year bonds; otherwise, SamsonGonzales would have to offer both bonds. So, VELSOR will offer 10-year bonds and SamsonGonzales will offer 5-year bonds. By Rule 1, HCN and Lorilou also offer one type of bond each, but the order cannot be determined. However, that leaves Goh Industrials and RST as the two corporations that offer both bond types.

5	10
H/L	L/H
S	V
G	G
R	R

The question asks for two corporations that could offer *only* 10-year bonds. Goh Industrials and RST offer both, not just 10-year bonds. That eliminates every choice but **(A)**, making that the correct answer. Sure enough, VELSOR does offer only 10-year bonds, and Lorilou could be the other such corporation.

22. (A) Could Be True
The correct answer will be a pair of corporations that could be the two that offer only 5-year bonds. The quickest way to answer this is to look at the sketch for the second question of the game. In that sketch, it's possible for SamsonGonzales to take up the final spot in the 10-year bonds column. In that case, Goh Industrials and HCN would be the two corporations that offer 5-year bonds, and only 5-year bonds. Because that outcome has been proven to be possible, that makes **(A)** the correct answer. For the record:

Rule 1 makes it such that HCN or Lorilou will be one of the corporations offering only 5-year bonds. So, the correct answer must include one of those corporations. That eliminates **(B)** and **(E)**. Further, HCN and Lorilou cannot offer the same bond type, which eliminates **(C)**. And if HCN offered 5-year bonds, then Lorilou would have to offer 10-year bonds (Rule 1), which would mean RST would also offer 10-year bonds (Rule 3). In that case, RST could *not* offer only 5-year bonds. That eliminates **(D)**.

23. (C) "If" / Must Be True
For this question, Goh Industrials and HCN will offer one bond type each, and they must be different. Whichever one HCN offers, Lorilou will offer the other (Rule 1), so Lorilou and Goh Industrials will offer the same bond type. However, it could go either way, so it will be worth drawing out both options.

In the first option, Goh Industrials (along with Lorilou) will offer 5-year bonds, with HCN offering 10-year bonds. For this question, Goh cannot offer both bonds, and Lorilou cannot offer both (Rule 1). So, neither one will offer 10-year bonds, which means the remaining four corporations must (HCN, RST, SamsonGonzales, VELSOR).

5	10
L	H
G	R
—	S
—	V

For the 5-year bonds, HCN is out (Rule 1). However, there are still three corporations (RST, SamsonGonzales, and VELSOR) that could take up the last two slots.

In the second option, Goh Industrials (along with Lorilou) will offer 10-year bonds. Again, neither of them offer both in this question, so neither offers 5-year bonds. That means, again, the remaining four corporations must (HCN, RST, SamsonGonzales, VELSOR). With Lorilou offering 10-year bonds, RST must, too (Rule 3). And with VELSOR offering 5-year bonds, SamsonGonzales must offer both and thus must take up the final slot in the 10-year bonds.

5	10
H	L
R	G
S	R
V	S

With two options in play, the correct answer must be true in *both* options. And that would be **(C)**. RST offers 10-year bonds in both options. Goh Industrials does not offer 10-year bonds in the first option, which eliminates **(A)**. VELSO does not offer 10-year bonds in the second option, which eliminates **(E)**. RST and VELSOR definitely offer 5-year bonds in the second option. However, in the first option, either one could offer 5-year bonds, but neither one has to for sure. That eliminates **(B)** and **(D)**.

Glossary

Logical Reasoning

Logical Reasoning Question Types

Argument-Based Questions

Main Point Question

A question that asks for an argument's conclusion or an author's main point. Typical question stems:

> Which one of the following most accurately expresses the conclusion of the argument as a whole?

> Which one of the following sentences best expresses the main point of the scientist's argument?

Role of a Statement Question

A question that asks how a specific sentence, statement, or idea functions within an argument. Typical question stems:

> Which one of the following most accurately describes the role played in the argument by the statement that automation within the steel industry allowed steel mills to produce more steel with fewer workers?

> The claim that governmental transparency is a nation's primary defense against public-sector corruption figures in the argument in which one of the following ways?

Point at Issue Question

A question that asks you to identify the specific claim, statement, or recommendation about which two speakers/authors disagree (or, rarely, about which they agree). Typical question stems:

> A point at issue between Tom and Jerry is

> The dialogue most strongly supports the claim that Marilyn and Billy disagree with each other about which one of the following?

Method of Argument Question

A question that asks you to describe an author's argumentative strategy. In other words, the correct answer describes *how* the author argues (not necessarily what the author says). Typical question stems:

> Which one of the following most accurately describes the technique of reasoning employed by the argument?

> Julian's argument proceeds by

> In the dialogue, Alexander responds to Abigail in which one of the following ways?

Parallel Reasoning Question

A question that asks you to identify the answer choice containing an argument that has the same logical structure and reaches the same type of conclusion as the argument in the stimulus does. Typical question stems:

> The pattern of reasoning in which one of the following arguments is most parallel to that in the argument above?

> The pattern of reasoning in which one of the following arguments is most similar to the pattern of reasoning in the argument above?

Assumption-Family Questions

Assumption Question

A question that asks you to identify one of the unstated premises in an author's argument. Assumption questions come in two varieties.

Necessary Assumption questions ask you to identify an unstated premise required for an argument's conclusion to follow logically from its evidence. Typical question stems:

> Which one of the following is an assumption on which the argument depends?

> Which one of the following is an assumption that the argument requires in order for its conclusion to be properly drawn?

Sufficient Assumption questions ask you to identify an unstated premise sufficient to establish the argument's conclusion on the basis of its evidence. Typical question stems:

> The conclusion follows logically if which one of the following is assumed?

> Which one of the following, if assumed, enables the conclusion above to be properly inferred?

Strengthen/Weaken Question

A question that asks you to identify a fact that, if true, would make the argument's conclusion more likely (Strengthen) or less likely (Weaken) to follow from its evidence. Typical question stems:

Strengthen

Which one of the following, if true, most strengthens the argument above?

Which one the following, if true, most strongly supports the claim above?

Weaken

Which one of the following, if true, would most weaken the argument above?

Which one of the following, if true, most calls into question the claim above?

Flaw Question

A question that asks you to describe the reasoning error that the author has made in an argument. Typical question stems:

The argument's reasoning is most vulnerable to criticism on the grounds that the argument

Which of the following identifies a reasoning error in the argument?

The reasoning in the correspondent's argument is questionable because the argument

Parallel Flaw Question

A question that asks you to identify the argument that contains the same error(s) in reasoning that the argument in the stimulus contains. Typical question stems:

The pattern of flawed reasoning exhibited by the argument above is most similar to that exhibited in which one of the following?

Which one of the following most closely parallels the questionable reasoning cited above?

Evaluate the Argument Question

A question that asks you to identify an issue or consideration relevant to the validity of an argument. Think of Evaluate questions as "Strengthen or Weaken" questions. The correct answer, if true, will strengthen the argument, and if false, will weaken the argument, or vice versa. Evaluate questions are very rare. Typical question stems:

Which one of the following would be most useful to know in order to evaluate the legitimacy of the professor's argument?

It would be most important to determine which one of the following in evaluating the argument?

Non-Argument Questions

Inference Question

A question that asks you to identify a statement that follows from the statements in the stimulus. It is very important to note the characteristics of the one correct and the four incorrect answers before evaluating the choices in Inference questions. Depending on the wording of the question stem, the correct answer to an Inference question may be the one that

- *must be true* if the statements in the stimulus are true

- is *most strongly supported* by the statements in the stimulus

- *must be false* if the statements in the stimulus are true

Typical question stems:

If all of the statements above are true, then which one of the following must also be true?

Which one of the following can be properly inferred from the information above?

If the statements above are true, then each of the following could be true EXCEPT:

Which one of the following is most strongly supported by the information above?

The statements above, if true, most support which one of the following?

The facts described above provide the strongest evidence against which one of the following?

Paradox Question

A question that asks you to identify a fact that, if true, most helps to explain, resolve, or reconcile an apparent contradiction. Typical question stems:

Which one of the following, if true, most helps to explain how both studies' findings could be accurate?

Which one the following, if true, most helps to resolve the apparent conflict in the spokesperson's statements?

Each one of the following, if true, would contribute to an explanation of the apparent discrepancy in the information above EXCEPT:

Principle Questions

Principle Question

A question that asks you to identify corresponding cases and principles. Some Principle questions provide a principle in the stimulus and call for the answer choice describing a case that corresponds to the principle. Others provide a specific case in the stimulus and call for the answer containing a principle to which that case corresponds.

On the LSAT, Principle questions almost always mirror the skills rewarded by other Logical Reasoning question types. After each of the following Principle question stems, we note the question type it resembles. Typical question stems:

> Which one of the following principles, if valid, most helps to justify the reasoning above? (**Strengthen**)

> Which one of the following most accurately expresses the principle underlying the reasoning above? (**Assumption**)

> The situation described above most closely conforms to which of the following generalizations? (**Inference**)

> Which one of the following situations conforms most closely to the principle described above? (**Inference**)

> Which one of the following principles, if valid, most helps to reconcile the apparent conflict among the prosecutor's claims? (**Paradox**)

Parallel Principle Question

A question that asks you to identify a specific case that illustrates the same principle that is illustrated by the case described in the stimulus. Typical question stem:

> Of the following, which one illustrates a principle that is most similar to the principle illustrated by the passage?

Untangling the Stimulus

Conclusion Types

The conclusions in arguments found in the Logical Reasoning section of the LSAT tend to fall into one of six categories:

1) Value Judgment (an evaluative statement; e.g., Action X is unethical, or Y's recital was poorly sung)

2) "If"/Then (a conditional prediction, recommendation, or assertion; e.g., If X is true, then so is Y, or If you are M, then you should do N)

3) Prediction (X *will* or *will not* happen in the future)

4) Comparison (X is taller/shorter/more common/less common, etc. than Y)

5) Assertion of Fact (X is true or X is false)

6) Recommendation (we *should* or *should not* do X)

One-Sentence Test

A tactic used to identify the author's conclusion in an argument. Consider which sentence in the argument is the one the author would keep if asked to get rid of everything except her main point.

Subsidiary Conclusion

A conclusion following from one piece of evidence and then used by the author to support his overall conclusion or main point. Consider the following argument:

> The pharmaceutical company's new experimental treatment did not succeed in clinical trials. As a result, the new treatment will not reach the market this year. Thus, the company will fall short of its revenue forecasts for the year.

Here, the sentence "As a result, the new treatment will not reach the market this year" is a subsidiary conclusion. It follows from the evidence that the new treatment failed in clinical trials, and it provides evidence for the overall conclusion that the company will not meet its revenue projections.

Keyword(s) in Logical Reasoning

A word or phrase that helps you untangle a question's stimulus by indicating the logical structure of the argument or the author's point. Here are three categories of Keywords to which LSAT experts pay special attention in Logical Reasoning:

Conclusion words; e.g., *therefore, thus, so, as a result, it follows that, consequently*, [evidence] *is evidence that* [conclusion]

Evidence word; e.g., *because, since, after all, for*, [evidence] *is evidence that* [conclusion]

Contrast words; e.g., *but, however, while, despite, in spite of, on the other hand* (These are especially useful in Paradox and Inference questions.)

Experts use Keywords even more extensively in Reading Comprehension. Learn the Keywords associated with the Reading Comprehension section, and apply them to Logical Reasoning when they are helpful.

Mismatched Concepts

One of two patterns to which authors' assumptions conform in LSAT arguments. Mismatched Concepts describes the assumption in arguments in which terms or concepts in the conclusion are different *in kind* from those in the evidence. The author assumes that there is a logical relationship between the different terms. For example:

> Bobby is a **championship swimmer**. Therefore, he **trains every day**.

Here, the words "trains every day" appear only in the conclusion, and the words "championship swimmer" appear only in the evidence. For the author to reach this conclusion from this evidence, he assumes that championship swimmers train every day.

Another example:

> Susan does **not eat her vegetables**. Thus, she will **not grow big and strong**.

In this argument, not growing big and strong is found only in the conclusion while not eating vegetables is found only in the evidence. For the author to reach this conclusion from this evidence, she must assume that eating one's vegetables is necessary for one to grow big and strong.

See also Overlooked Possibilities.

Overlooked Possibilities

One of two patterns to which authors' assumptions conform in LSAT arguments. Overlooked Possibilities describes the assumption in arguments in which terms or concepts in the conclusion are different *in degree, scale, or level of certainty* from those in the evidence. The author assumes that there is no factor or explanation for the conclusion other than the one(s) offered in the evidence. For example:

> Samson does not have a ticket stub for this movie showing. Thus, Samson must have sneaked into the movie without paying.

The author assumes that there is no other explanation for Samson's lack of a ticket stub. The author overlooks several possibilities: e.g., Samson had a special pass for this showing of the movie; Samson dropped his ticket stub by accident or threw it away after entering the theater; someone else in Samson's party has all of the party members' ticket stubs in her pocket or handbag.

Another example:

> Jonah's marketing plan will save the company money. Therefore, the company should adopt Jonah's plan.

Here, the author makes a recommendation based on one advantage. The author assumes that the advantage is the company's only concern or that there are no disadvantages that could outweigh it, e.g., Jonah's plan might save money on marketing but not generate any new leads or customers; Jonah's plan might damage the company's image or reputation; Jonah's plan might include illegal false advertising. Whenever the author of an LSAT argument concludes with a recommendation or a prediction based on just a single fact in the evidence, that author is always overlooking many other possibilities.

See also Mismatched Concepts.

Causal Argument

An argument in which the author concludes or assumes that one thing causes another. The most common pattern on the LSAT is for the author to conclude that A causes B from evidence that A and B are correlated. For example:

> I notice that whenever the store has a poor sales month, employee tardiness is also higher that month. Therefore, it must be that employee tardiness causes the store to lose sales.

The author assumes that the correlation in the evidence indicates a causal relationship. These arguments are vulnerable to three types of overlooked possibilities:

1) There could be **another causal factor**. In the previous example, maybe the months in question are those in which the manager takes vacation, causing the store to lose sales and permitting employees to arrive late without fear of the boss's reprimands.

2) Causation could be **reversed**. Maybe in months when sales are down, employee morale suffers and tardiness increases as a result.

3) The correlation could be **coincidental**. Maybe the correlation between tardiness and the dip in sales is pure coincidence.

See also Flaw Types: Correlation versus Causation.

Another pattern in causal arguments (less frequent on the LSAT) involves the assumption that a particular causal mechanism is or is not involved in a causal relationship. For example:

> The airport has rerouted takeoffs and landings so that they will not create noise over the Sunnyside neighborhood. Thus, the recent drop in Sunnyside's property values cannot be explained by the neighborhood's proximity to the airport.

Here, the author assumes that the only way that the airport could be the cause of dropping property values is through noise pollution. The author overlooks any other possible mechanism (e.g., frequent traffic jams and congestion) through which proximity to the airport could be the cause of Sunnyside's woes.

Principle

A broad, law-like rule, definition, or generalization that covers a variety of specific cases with defined attributes. To see how principles are treated on the LSAT, consider the following principle:

> It is immoral for a person for his own gain to mislead another person.

That principle would cover a specific case, such as a seller who lies about the quality of construction to get a higher price for his house. It would also correspond to the case of a teenager who, wishing to spend a night out on the town, tells his mom "I'm going over to Randy's house." He knows that his mom believes that he will be staying at Randy's house, when in fact, he and Randy will go out together.

That principle does not, however, cover cases in which someone lies solely for the purpose of making the other person feel better or in which one person inadvertently misleads the other through a mistake of fact.

Be careful not to apply your personal ethics or morals when analyzing the principles articulated on the test.

Flaw Types

Necessary versus Sufficient

This flaw occurs when a speaker or author concludes that one event is necessary for a second event from evidence that the first event is sufficient to bring about the second event, or vice versa. Example:

> If more than 25,000 users attempt to access the new app at the same time, the server will crash. Last night, at 11:15 PM, the server crashed, so it must be the case that more than 25,000 users were attempting to use the new app at that time.

In making this argument, the author assumes that the only thing that will cause the server to crash is the usage level (i.e., high usage is *necessary* for the server to crash). The evidence, however, says that high usage is one thing that will cause the server to crash (i.e., that high usage is *sufficient* to crash the server).

Correlation versus Causation

This flaw occurs when a speaker or author draws a conclusion that one thing causes another from evidence that the two things are correlated. Example:

> Over the past half century, global sugar consumption has tripled. That same time period has seen a surge in the rate of technological advancement worldwide. It follows that the increase in sugar consumption has caused the acceleration in technological advancement.

In any argument with this structure, the author is making three unwarranted assumptions. First, he assumes that there is no alternate cause, i.e., there is nothing else that has contributed to rapid technological advancement. Second, he assumes that the causation is not reversed, i.e., technological advancement has not contributed to the increase in sugar consumption, perhaps by making it easier to grow, refine, or transport sugar. And, third, he assumes that the two phenomena are not merely coincidental, i.e., that it is not just happenstance that global sugar consumption is up at the same time that the pace of technological advancement has accelerated.

Unrepresentative Sample

This flaw occurs when a speaker or author draws a conclusion about a group from evidence in which the sample cannot represent that group because the sample is too small or too selective, or is biased in some way. Example:

> Moviegoers in our town prefer action films and romantic comedies over other film genres. Last Friday, we sent reporters to survey moviegoers at several theaters in town, and nearly 90 percent of those surveyed were going to watch either an action film or a romantic comedy.

The author assumes that the survey was representative of the town's moviegoers, but there are several reasons to question that assumption. First, we don't know how many people were actually surveyed. Even if the number of people surveyed was adequate, we don't know how many other types of movies were playing. Finally, the author doesn't limit her conclusion to moviegoers on Friday nights. If the survey had been conducted at Sunday matinees, maybe most moviegoers would have been heading out to see an animated family film or a historical drama. Who knows?

Scope Shift/Unwarranted Assumption

This flaw occurs when a speaker's or author's evidence has a scope or has terms different enough from the scope or terms in his conclusion that it is doubtful that the evidence can support the conclusion. Example:

> A very small percentage of working adults in this country can correctly define collateralized debt obligation securities. Thus, sad to say, the majority of the nation's working adults cannot make prudent choices about how to invest their savings.

This speaker assumes that prudent investing requires the ability to accurately define a somewhat obscure financial term. But prudence is not the same thing as expertise, and the speaker does not offer any evidence that this knowledge of this particular term is related to wise investing.

Percent versus Number/Rate versus Number

This flaw occurs when a speaker or author draws a conclusion about real quantities from evidence about rates or percentages, or vice versa. Example:

> At the end of last season, Camp SunnyDay laid off half of their senior counselors and a quarter of their junior counselors. Thus, Camp SunnyDay must have more senior counselors than junior counselors.

The problem, of course, is that we don't know how many senior and junior counselors were on staff before the layoffs. If there were a total of 4 senior counselors and 20 junior counselors, then the camp would have laid off only 2 senior counselors while dismissing 5 junior counselors.

Equivocation

This flaw occurs when a speaker or author uses the same word in two different and incompatible ways. Example:

> Our opponent in the race has accused our candidate's staff members of behaving unprofessionally. But that's not fair. Our staff is made up entirely of volunteers, not paid campaign workers.

The speaker interprets the opponent's use of the word *professional* to mean "paid," but the opponent likely meant something more along the lines of "mature, competent, and businesslike."

Ad Hominem

This flaw occurs when a speaker or author concludes that another person's claim or argument is invalid because that other person has a personal flaw or shortcoming. One common pattern is for the speaker or author to claim the other person acts hypocritically or that the other person's claim is made from self-interest. Example:

> Mrs. Smithers testified before the city council, stating that the speed limits on the residential streets near her home are dangerously high. But why should we give her claim any credence? The way she eats and exercises, she's not even looking out for her own health.

The author attempts to undermine Mrs. Smithers's testimony by attacking her character and habits. He doesn't offer any evidence that is relevant to her claim about speed limits.

Part versus Whole

This flaw occurs when a speaker or author concludes that a part or individual has a certain characteristic because the whole or the larger group has that characteristic, or vice versa. Example:

> Patient: I should have no problems taking the three drugs prescribed to me by my doctors. I looked them up, and none of the three is listed as having any major side effects.

Here, the patient is assuming that what is true of each of the drugs individually will be true of them when taken together. The patient's flaw is overlooking possible interactions that could cause problems not present when the drugs are taken separately.

Circular Reasoning

This flaw occurs when a speaker or author tries to prove a conclusion with evidence that is logically equivalent to the conclusion. Example:

> All those who run for office are prevaricators. To see this, just consider politicians: they all prevaricate.

Perhaps the author has tried to disguise the circular reasoning in this argument by exchanging the words "those who run for office" in the conclusion for "politicians" in the evidence, but all this argument amounts to is "Politicians prevaricate; therefore, politicians prevaricate." On the LSAT, circular reasoning is very rarely the correct answer to a Flaw question, although it is regularly described in one of the wrong answers.

Question Strategies

Denial Test

A tactic for identifying the assumption *necessary* to an argument. When you negate an assumption necessary to an argument, the argument will fall apart. Negating an assumption that is not necessary to the argument will not invalidate the argument. Consider the following argument:

> Only high schools that produced a state champion athlete during the school year will be represented at the Governor's awards banquet. Therefore, McMurtry High School will be represented at the Governor's awards banquet.

Which one of the following is an assumption necessary to that argument?

> (1) McMurtry High School produced more state champion athletes than any other high school during the school year.

> (2) McMurtry High School produced at least one state champion athlete during the school year.

If you are at all confused about which of those two statements reflects the *necessary* assumption, negate them both.

> (1) McMurtry High School **did not produce more** state champion athletes than any other high school during the school year.

That does not invalidate the argument. McMurtry could still be represented at the Governor's banquet.

> (2) McMurtry High School **did not produce any** state champion athletes during the school year.

Here, negating the statement causes the argument to fall apart. Statement (2) is an assumption *necessary* to the argument.

Point at Issue "Decision Tree"

A tactic for evaluating the answer choices in Point at Issue questions. The correct answer is the only answer choice to which you can answer "Yes" to all three questions in the following diagram.

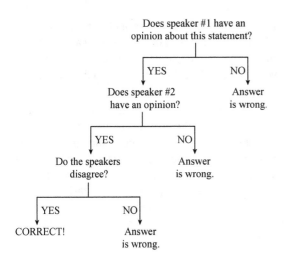

Common Methods of Argument

These methods of argument or argumentative strategies are common on the LSAT:

- Analogy, in which an author draws parallels between two unrelated (but purportedly similar) situations
- Example, in which an author cites a specific case or cases to justify a generalization
- Counterexample, in which an author seeks to discredit an opponent's argument by citing a specific case or cases that appear to invalidate the opponent's generalization
- Appeal to authority, in which an author cites an expert's claim or opinion as support for her conclusion
- Ad hominem attack, in which an author attacks her opponent's personal credibility rather than attacking the substance of her opponent's argument
- Elimination of alternatives, in which an author lists possibilities and discredits or rules out all but one
- Means/requirements, in which the author argues that something is needed to achieve a desired result

Wrong Answer Types in LR

Outside the Scope (Out of Scope; Beyond the Scope)

An answer choice containing a statement that is too broad, too narrow, or beyond the purview of the stimulus, making the statement in the choice irrelevant

180

An answer choice that directly contradicts what the correct answer must say (e.g., a choice that strengthens the argument in a Weaken question)

Extreme

An answer choice containing language too emphatic to be supported by the stimulus; often (although not always) characterized by words such as *all*, *never*, *every*, *only*, or *most*

Distortion

An answer choice that mentions details from the stimulus but mangles or misstates what the author said about those details

Irrelevant Comparison

An answer choice that compares two items or attributes in a way not germane to the author's argument or statements

Half-Right/Half-Wrong

An answer choice that begins correctly, but then contradicts or distorts the passage in its second part; this wrong answer type is more common in Reading Comprehension than it is in Logical Reasoning

Faulty Use of Detail

An answer choice that accurately states something from the stimulus, but does so in a manner that answers the question incorrectly; this wrong answer type is more common in Reading Comprehension than it is in Logical Reasoning

Logic Games

Game Types

Strict Sequencing Game

A game that asks you to arrange entities into numbered positions or into a set schedule (usually hours or days). Strict Sequencing is, by far, the most common game type on the LSAT. In the typical Strict Sequencing game, there is a one-to-one matchup of entities and positions, e.g., seven entities to be placed in seven positions, one per position, or six entities to be placed over six consecutive days, one entity per day.

From time to time, the LSAT will offer Strict Sequencing with more entities than positions (e.g., seven entities to be arranged over five days, with some days to receive more than one entity) or more positions than entities (e.g., six entities to be scheduled over seven days, with at least one day to receive no entities).

Other, less common variations on Strict Sequencing include:

Double Sequencing, in which each entity is placed or scheduled two times (there have been rare occurrences of Triple or Quadruple Sequencing). Alternatively, a Double Sequencing game may involve two different sets of entities each sequenced once.

Circular Sequencing, in which entities are arranged around a table or in a circular arrangement (NOTE: When the positions in a Circular Sequencing game are numbered, the first and last positions are adjacent.)

Vertical Sequencing, in which the positions are numbered from top to bottom or from bottom to top (as in the floors of a building)

Loose Sequencing Game

A game that asks you to arrange or schedule entities in order but provides no numbering or naming of the positions. The rules in Loose Sequencing give only the relative positions (earlier or later, higher or lower) between two entities or among three entities. Loose Sequencing games almost always provide that there will be no ties between entities in the rank, order, or position they take.

Circular Sequencing Game

See Strict Sequencing Game.

Selection Game

A game that asks you to choose or include some entities from the initial list of entities and to reject or exclude others. Some Selection games provide overall limitations on the number of entities to be selected (e.g., "choose exactly four of seven students" or "choose at least two of six entrees") while others provide little or no restriction on the number selected ("choose at least one type of flower" or "select from among seven board members").

Distribution Game

A game that asks you to break up the initial list of entities into two, three, or (very rarely) four groups or teams. In the vast majority of Distribution games, each entity is assigned to one and only one group or team. A relatively common variation on Distribution games will provide a subdivided list of entities (e.g., eight students—four men and four women—will form three study groups) and will then require representatives from those subdivisions on each team (e.g., each study group will have at least one of the men on it).

Matching Game

A game that asks you to match one or more members of one set of entities to specific members of another set of entities, or that asks you to match attributes or objects to a set of entities. Unlike Distribution games, in which each entity is placed in exactly one group or team, Matching games usually permit you to assign the same attribute or object to more than one entity.

In some cases, there are overall limitations on the number of entities that can be matched (e.g., "In a school's wood shop, there are four workstations—numbered 1 through 4—and each workstation has at least one and at most three of the following tools—band saw, dremmel tool, electric sander, and power drill"). In almost all Matching games, further restrictions on the number of entities that can be matched to a particular person or place will be found in the rules (e.g., Workstation 4 will have more tools than Workstation 2 has).

Hybrid Game

A game that asks you to do two (or rarely, three) of the standard actions (Sequencing, Selection, Distribution, and Matching) to a set of entities.

The most common Hybrid is Sequencing-Matching. A typical Sequencing-Matching Hybrid game might ask you to schedule six speakers at a conference to six one-hour speaking slots (from 9 AM to 2 PM), and then assign each speaker one of two subjects (economic development or trade policy).

Nearly as common as Sequencing-Matching is Distribution-Sequencing. A typical game of this type might ask you to divide six people in a talent competition into either a Dance category or a Singing category, and then rank the competitors in each category.

It is most common to see one Hybrid game in each Logic Games section, although there have been tests with two Hybrid games and tests with none. To determine the type of Hybrid you are faced with, identify the game's action in Step 1 of the Logic Games Method. For example, a game asking you to choose four of six runners, and then assign the four chosen runners to lanes numbered 1 through 4 on a track, would be a Selection-Sequencing Hybrid game.

Mapping Game

A game that provides you with a description of geographical locations and, typically, of the connections among them. Mapping games often ask you to determine the shortest possible routes between two locations or to account for the number of connections required to travel from one location to another. This game type is extremely rare, and as of February 2017, a Mapping game was last seen on PrepTest 40 administered in June 2003.

Process Game

A game that opens with an initial arrangement of entities (e.g., a starting sequence or grouping) and provides rules that describe the processes through which that arrangement can be altered. The questions typically ask you for acceptable arrangements or placements of particular entities after one, two, or three stages in the process. Occasionally, a Process game question might provide information about the arrangement after one, two, or three stages in the process and ask you what must have happened in the earlier stages. This game type is extremely rare, and as of November 2016, a Process game was last seen on PrepTest 16 administered in September 1995. However, there was a Process game on PrepTest 80, administered in December 2016, thus ending a 20-year hiatus.

Game Setups and Deductions

Floater

An entity that is not restricted by any rule or limitation in the game

Blocks of Entities

Two or more entities that are required by rule to be adjacent or separated by a set number of spaces (Sequencing games), to be placed together in the same group (Distribution games), to be matched to the same entity (Matching games), or to be selected or rejected together (Selection games)

Limited Options

Rules or restrictions that force all of a game's acceptable arrangements into two (or occasionally three) patterns

Established Entities

An entity required by rule to be placed in one space or assigned to one particular group throughout the entire game

Number Restrictions

Rules or limitations affecting the number of entities that may be placed into a group or space throughout the game

Duplications

Two or more rules that restrict a common entity. Usually, these rules can be combined to reach additional deductions. For example, if you know that B is placed earlier than A in a sequence and that C is placed earlier than B in that sequence, you can deduce that C is placed earlier than A in the sequence and that there is at least one space (the space occupied by B) between C and A.

Master Sketch

The final sketch derived from the game's setup, rules, and deductions. LSAT experts preserve the Master Sketch for reference as they work through the questions. The Master Sketch does not include any conditions from New-"If" question stems.

Logic Games Question Types

Acceptability Question

A question in which the correct answer is an acceptable arrangement of all the entities relative to the spaces, groups, or selection criteria in the game. Answer these by using the rules to eliminate answer choices that violate the rules.

Partial Acceptability Question

A question in which the correct answer is an acceptable arrangement of some of the entities relative to some of the spaces, groups, or selection criteria in the game, and in which the arrangement of entities not included in the answer choices could be acceptable to the spaces, groups, or selection criteria not explicitly shown in the answer choices. Answer these the same way you would answer Acceptability questions, by using the rules to eliminate answer choices that explicitly or implicitly violate the rules.

Must Be True/False; Could Be True/False Question

A question in which the correct answer must be true, could be true, could be false, or must be false (depending on the question stem), and in which no additional rules or conditions are provided by the question stem

New-"If" Question

A question in which the stem provides an additional rule, condition, or restriction (applicable only to that question), and then asks what must/could be true/false as a result. LSAT experts typically handle New-"If" questions by copying the Master Sketch, adding the new restriction to the copy, and working out any additional deductions available as a result of the new restriction before evaluating the answer choices.

Rule Substitution Question

A question in which the correct answer is a rule that would have an impact identical to one of the game's original rules on the entities in the game

Rule Change Question

A question in which the stem alters one of the original rules in the game, and then asks what must/could be true/false as a result. LSAT experts typically handle Rule Change questions by reconstructing the game's sketch, but now accounting for the changed rule in place of the original. These questions are rare on recent tests.

Rule Suspension Question

A question in which the stem indicates that you should ignore one of the original rules in the game, and then asks what must/could be true/false as a result. LSAT experts typically handle Rule Suspension questions by reconstructing the game's sketch, but now accounting for the absent rule. These questions are very rare.

Complete and Accurate List Question

A question in which the correct answer is a list of any and all entities that could acceptably appear in a particular space or group, or a list of any and all spaces or groups in which a particular entity could appear

Completely Determine Question

A question in which the correct answer is a condition that would result in exactly one acceptable arrangement for all of the entities in the game

Supply the "If" Question

A question in which the correct answer is a condition that would guarantee a particular result stipulated in the question stem

Minimum/Maximum Question

A question in which the correct answer is the number corresponding to the fewest or greatest number of entities that could be selected (Selection), placed into a particular group (Distribution), or matched to a particular entity (Matching). Often, Minimum/Maximum questions begin with New-"If" conditions.

Earliest/Latest Question

A question in which the correct answer is the earliest or latest position in which an entity may acceptably be placed. Often, Earliest/Latest questions begin with New-"If" conditions.

"How Many" Question

A question in which the correct answer is the exact number of entities that may acceptably be placed into a particular group or space. Often, "How Many" questions begin with New-"If" conditions.

Reading Comprehension

Strategic Reading

Roadmap

The test taker's markup of the passage text in Step 1 (Read the Passage Strategically) of the Reading Comprehension Method. To create helpful Roadmaps, LSAT experts circle or underline Keywords in the passage text and jot down brief, helpful notes or paragraph summaries in the margin of their test booklets.

Keyword(s) in Reading Comprehension

Words in the passage text that reveal the passage structure or the author's point of view and thus help test takers anticipate and research the questions that accompany the passage. LSAT experts pay attention to six categories of Keywords in Reading Comprehension:

Emphasis/Opinion—words that signal that the author finds a detail noteworthy or that the author has positive or negative opinion about a detail; any subjective or evaluative language on the author's part (e.g., *especially, crucial, unfortunately, disappointing, I suggest, it seems likely*)

Contrast—words indicating that the author finds two details or ideas incompatible or that the two details illustrate conflicting points (e.g., *but, yet, despite, on the other hand*)

Logic—words that indicate an argument, either the author's or someone else's; these include both Evidence and Conclusion Keywords (e.g., *thus, therefore, because, it follows that*)

Illustration—words indicating an example offered to clarify or support another point (e.g., *for example, this shows, to illustrate*)

Sequence/Chronology—words showing steps in a process or developments over time (e.g., *traditionally, in the past, today, first, second, finally, earlier, subsequent*)

Continuation—words indicating that a subsequent example or detail supports the same point or illustrates the same idea as the previous example (e.g., *moreover, in addition, also, further, along the same lines*)

Margin Notes

The brief notes or paragraph summaries that the test taker jots down next to the passage in the margin of the test booklet

Big Picture Summaries: Topic/Scope/Purpose/Main Idea

A test taker's mental summary of the passage as a whole made during Step 1 (Read the Passage Strategically) of the Reading Comprehension Method. LSAT experts account for four aspects of the passage in their big picture summaries:

Topic—the overall subject of the passage

Scope—the particular aspect of the Topic that the author focuses on

Purpose—the author's reason or motive for writing the passage (express this as a verb; e.g., *to refute, to outline, to evaluate, to critique*)

Main Idea—the author's conclusion or overall takeaway; if the passage does not contain an explicit conclusion or thesis, you can combine the author's Scope and Purpose to get a good sense of the Main Idea.

Passage Types

Kaplan categorizes Reading Comprehension passages in two ways, by subject matter and by passage structure.

Subject matter categories

In the majority of LSAT Reading Comprehension sections, there is one passage from each of the following subject matter categories:

Humanities—topics from art, music, literature, philosophy, etc.

Natural Science—topics from biology, astronomy, paleontology, physics, etc.

Social Science—topics from anthropology, history, sociology, psychology, etc.

Law—topics from constitutional law, international law, legal education, jurisprudence, etc.

Passage structure categories

The majority of LSAT Reading Comprehension passages correspond to one of the following descriptions. The first categories—Theory/Perspective and Event/Phenomenon—have been the most common on recent LSATs.

Theory/Perspective—The passage focuses on a thinker's theory or perspective on some aspect of the Topic; typically (though not always), the author disagrees and critiques the thinker's perspective and/or defends his own perspective.

Event/Phenomenon—The passage focuses on an event, a breakthrough development, or a problem that has recently arisen; when a solution to the problem is proposed, the author most often agrees with the solution (and that represents the passage's Main Idea).

Biography—The passage discusses something about a notable person; the aspect of the person's life emphasized by the author reflects the Scope of the passage.

Debate—The passage outlines two opposing positions (neither of which is the author's) on some aspect of the Topic; the author may side with one of the positions, may remain neutral, or may critique both. (This structure has been relatively rare on recent LSATs.)

Comparative Reading

A pair of passages (labeled Passage A and Passage B) that stand in place of the typical single passage; they have appeared exactly one time in each Reading Comprehension section administered since June 2007. The paired Comparative Reading passages share the same Topic, but may have different Scopes and Purposes. On most LSAT tests, a majority of the questions accompanying Comparative Reading passages require the test taker to compare or contrast ideas or details from both passages.

Question Strategies

Research Clues

A reference in a Reading Comprehension question stem to a word, phrase, or detail in the passage text, or to a particular line number or paragraph in the passage. LSAT experts recognize five kinds of research clues:

Line Reference—An LSAT expert researches around the referenced lines, looking for Keywords that indicate why the referenced details were included or how they were used by the author.

Paragraph Reference—An LSAT expert consults her passage Roadmap to see the paragraph's Scope and Purpose.

Quoted Text (often accompanied by a line reference)—An LSAT expert checks the context of the quoted term or phrase, asking what the author meant by it in the passage.

Proper Nouns—An LSAT expert checks the context of the person, place, or thing in the passage, asking whether the author made a positive, negative, or neutral evaluation of it and why the author included it in the passage.

Content Clues—These are terms, concepts, or ideas from the passage mentioned in the question stem but not as direct quotes and not accompanied by line references. An LSAT expert knows that content clues almost always refer to something that the author emphasized or about which the author expressed an opinion.

Reading Comp Question Types

Global Question

A question that asks for the Main Idea of the passage or for the author's primary Purpose in writing the passage. Typical question stems:

> Which one of the following most accurately expresses the main point of the passage?

> The primary purpose of the passage is to

Detail Question

A question that asks what the passage explicitly states about a detail. Typical question stems:

> According to the passage, some critics have criticized Gilliam's films on the grounds that

> The passage states that one role of a municipality's comptroller in budget decisions by the city council is to

> The author identifies which one of the following as a commonly held but false preconception?

> The passage contains sufficient information to answer which of the following questions?

Occasionally, the test will ask for a correct answer that contains a detail *not* stated in the passage:

> The author attributes each of the following positions to the Federalists EXCEPT:

Inference Question

A question that asks for a statement that follows from or is based on the passage but that is not necessarily stated explicitly in the passage. Some Inference questions contain research clues. The following are typical Inference question stems containing research clues:

> Based on the passage, the author would be most likely to agree with which one of the following statements about unified field theory?

> The passage suggests which one of the following about the behavior of migratory water fowl?

> Given the information in the passage, to which one of the following would radiocarbon dating techniques likely be applicable?

Other Inference questions lack research clues in the question stem. They may be evaluated using the test taker's Big Picture Summaries, or the answer choices may make it clear that the test taker should research a particular part of the passage text. The following are typical Inference question stems containing research clues:

> It can be inferred from the passage that the author would be most likely to agree that

> Which one of the following statements is most strongly supported by the passage?

Other Reading Comprehension question types categorized as Inference questions are Author's Attitude questions and Vocabulary-in-Context questions.

Logic Function Question

A question that asks why the author included a particular detail or reference in the passage or how the author used a particular detail or reference. Typical question stems:

> The author of the passage mentions declining inner-city populations in the paragraph most likely in order to

> The author's discussion of Rimbaud's travels in the Mediterranean (lines 23–28) functions primarily to

> Which one of the following best expresses the function of the third paragraph in the passage?

Logic Reasoning Question

A question that asks the test taker to apply Logical Reasoning skills in relation to a Reading Comprehension passage. Logic Reasoning questions often mirror Strengthen or Parallel Reasoning questions, and occasionally mirror Method of Argument or Principle questions. Typical question stems:

> Which one of the following, if true, would most strengthen the claim made by the author in the last sentence of the passage (lines 51–55)?

> Which one of the following pairs of proposals is most closely analogous to the pair of studies discussed in the passage?

Author's Attitude Question

A question that asks for the author's opinion or point of view on the subject discussed in the passage or on a detail mentioned in the passage. Since the correct answer may follow from the passage without being explicitly stated in it, some Author's Attitude questions are characterized as a subset of Inference questions. Typical question stems:

> The author's attitude toward the use of DNA evidence in the appeals by convicted felons is most accurately described as

> The author's stance regarding monetarist economic theories can most accurately be described as one of

Vocabulary-in-Context Question

A question that asks how the author uses a word or phrase within the context of the passage. The word or phrase in question is always one with multiple meanings. Since the correct answer follows from its use in the passage, Vocabulary-in-Context questions are characterized as a subset of Inference questions. Typical question stems:

> Which one of the following is closest in meaning to the word "citation" as it used in the second paragraph of the passage (line 18)?

> In context, the word "enlightenment" (line 24) refers to

Wrong Answer Types in RC

Outside the Scope (Out of Scope; Beyond the Scope)

An answer choice containing a statement that is too broad, too narrow, or beyond the purview of the passage

180

An answer choice that directly contradicts what the correct answer must say

Extreme

An answer choice containing language too emphatic (e.g., *all*, *never*, *every*, *none*) to be supported by the passage

Distortion

An answer choice that mentions details or ideas from the passage but mangles or misstates what the author said about those details or ideas

Faulty Use of Detail

An answer choice that accurately states something from the passage but in a manner that incorrectly answers the question

Half-Right/Half-Wrong

An answer choice in which one clause follows from the passage while another clause contradicts or deviates from the passage

Contrapositive

The conditional statement logically equivalent to another conditional statement formed by reversing the order of and negating the terms in the original conditional statement. For example, reversing and negating the terms in this statement:

$$\textit{If} \quad \textit{A} \qquad \rightarrow \quad \textit{B}$$

results in its contrapositive:

$$\textit{If} \quad \sim\!\textit{B} \qquad \rightarrow \quad \sim\!\textit{A}$$

To form the contrapositive of conditional statements in which either the sufficient clause or the necessary clause has more than one term, you must also change the conjunction *and* to *or*, or vice versa. For example, reversing and negating the terms and changing *and* to *or* in this statement:

$$\textit{If} \quad \textit{M} \qquad \rightarrow \quad \textit{O AND P}$$

results in its contrapositive:

$$\textit{If} \quad \sim\!\textit{O OR} \sim\!\textit{P} \qquad \rightarrow \quad \sim\!\textit{M}$$

Formal Logic Terms

Conditional Statement ("If"-Then Statement)

A statement containing a sufficient clause and a necessary clause. Conditional statements can be described in Formal Logic shorthand as:

If [*sufficient clause*] $\rightarrow$ [*necessary clause*]

In some explanations, the LSAT expert may refer to the sufficient clause as the statement's "trigger" and to the necessary clause as the statement's result.

For more on how to interpret, describe, and use conditional statements on the LSAT, please refer to "A Note About Formal Logic on the LSAT" in this book's introduction.

Printed in the USA
CPSIA information can be obtained
at www.ICGtesting.com
LVHW010205301023
762520LV00022B/389